Chosen for such a time
as NOW. Step into
your prophetic role.

Not Cheated,
but Chosen

DESMICIA CALHOUN

Books may be purchased by contacting the author at:
www.chosennotcheated.com

Cover Design: Candice Kilgore
Cover Image: Carlous Mack
Publisher: Desmicia Calhoun
Edited and Printed by: Rocky Heights Print and Binding Inc.

Printed in the United States

Printing Number 10 9 8 7 6 5 4 3 2 1

Dedication

To my niece:

As I began to write this book and think about who I wanted to read it, you rose to the top of my list. More than anyone else in my life, I want YOU to know that you were not cheated. You were CHOSEN by God. I remember three important phone calls in reference to you. The first one came from a family member letting me know that I had a niece on the way. I was stationed at Fort Campbell, Kentucky, at the time. I didn't know many details, but I was happy and ready to be the best auntie in the world. The second one came on the day you were born. Your mother was having issues, and you were in distress, so, they called to say that the doctor was about to do an emergency C-section. Dang, I was expected to come home for Christmas and was hoping you would wait for me; but I prayed for a healthy baby and waited on the follow-up. The third call came December 31, 2014, from my brother. He said a paternity test had revealed that you were not his child. I want you to know that I loved you the same on all three calls. I love you today, and I will never stop loving you.

Despite the worldly circumstances, I know that you were chosen for us during a time when we felt cheated. Losing our mom in a car accident in 2003 was hard on us. Although we didn't share much with each other verbally, we shared the same pain internally. YOU filled the hole in our hearts and tied us together in an extraordinary way. I anticipated your arrival. I remember seeing the first picture of you and joking about you having a big nose like him. I remember asking them what your name was, and my brother replied, "I don't know. I guess she will write something down on that paper when they bring it in there." Your daddy gave you your first name after our cousin. I gave you your middle name, La Honey, after our mom. I remember holding you for the first time and seeing my mother in your eyes. At that moment, I knew you had the perfect name. When the angels dropped you off on December 19, 2006, you brought a piece of my mother back with you.

I see the hand of God on your life. It's been there since you were born. You didn't enter our family by mistake or coincidence; you were CHOSEN to bring us joy and soften our hard hearts with your authentic love. You came in the world weighing only 4 pounds and 7 ounces, but you've always been my tiny giant. You are humble, caring, talented and loving. I know your call comes with devils you will have to slay. If I don't live long enough to slay them with you, I hope that my story gives you strength to walk boldly in your purpose. I dedicate this book to you. Thank you for being my angel.

With Love,
Auntie Micia

Contents

Acknowledgements

To God:

Thank you for not only choosing me, but for equipping me for this call. Thank you for pouring into me as I poured into these pages. May your words travel everywhere you ordered them to and touch the lives of your people in only a way that you can. Thank you for not giving up on me and loving me unconditionally.

To my children, Honey and Nolan:

Thank you for motivating me to become a better version of me daily. Thank you for keeping me humble and hungry for success.

To my family and friends:

Thank you for always supporting me in my career, my parenting, and my life. Whether you kept my kids to give me time to write or simply encouraged me along the way, I could not have completed this task without you all on my team.

To Pastor Tonya Chestnut:

Thank you for fulfilling your assignment to me. Thank you for seeing me before I saw me and pushing me past my self-imposed limits. May God continue to bless your family.

Chapter One
Not Cheated, but Chosen

H ave you lost a parent, spouse, sibling, or child? Experienced a horrible heartbreak? Recently divorced? Raising a child alone? Molested or abused as a child? Not raised in the traditional family? Feeling isolated and unworthy? Living with physical limitations? Suffering from health issues? These and many other issues can have you feeling cheated. I know, because I felt cheated for years. I thought that every bad thing that I experienced came from the devil and every good thing came from God, and for some reason, the bad things always stuck out to me. In the midst of some of my highest achievements, I was reminded of painful losses.

I remember arriving at Fort Jackson, South Carolina, for Army Basic Training on August 24, 2005. The first few days were in-processing, and I was so excited to finally get my uniform. As we went through the line, a lady gave us a set to try on in front of a tall mirror on the wall. I will never forget bursting into tears as I looked at myself for the first time as a Soldier. Everyone around me thought I was just homesick, but in reality, I was looking at a reflection of my mom in the mirror. They had no idea that seeing myself in the uniform reminded me of my deceased mother who had worn this uniform in the Alabama Army National Guard. As proud as I was to continue her legacy, I felt cheated out of her getting to see me take the torch.

I used to allow the enemy to insert a painful memory into every happy moment in my life until I realized who I was. If this is you, let me talk to you. Jeremiah 1: 5 reads: *"Before I formed you in your mother's womb,* **I chose you**. *Before you were born, I set you apart. I appointed you to be a prophet to the nations."* It does not matter if you were unplanned or born under unfavorable circumstances. **He chose you**. It is okay that you may have felt unwanted as a child. **He chose you**. It is okay if you felt like the odd person or black sheep of your family. I remember feeling like my mother loved my brother more than she loved me. It hurt her heart when I expressed to her that I felt that way. I remember she cried and tried to explain. It wasn't until I was older that I realized that she loved us the same, but we required a different kind of love. Even though he is older, he was mild-tempered and very attached to her. I was the younger, strong-willed one who required tough love.

As a mother who birthed us, she knew each of us the same way that God created and chose each of us. He chose you and me to be prophets to the nations, so, don't ever let the devil make you feel like you can't be the one. You were created by the Almighty One. I am here to stand with you and serve notice to the enemy that the feeling of being cheated ends today. All those feelings, events, and circumstances that you endured were all part of God's plan for your life, so, understand this—**you were not cheated; you were chosen.**

I once heard a pastor say, "You can't heal what you won't reveal." Although it sounded so cliché, it hit home; so, let me help myself before I help you. Truth is, I went through years of hidden pain, because I refused to reveal the fact that I felt cheated. Like you, I was on what felt like a meaningless and exhausting chase for this thing called "purpose". The thing is, I could not define 'my purpose'. All I knew was that I was supposed to have one. I was so irritated with the failing pursuit until one day I googled the word 'purpose'. It means to pursue, chase, follow, trail or go after something or someone; and, I asked myself, "What is it supposed to look or feel like? How will I know when I get there?" My purpose could not have been to go through life on this wild goose chase for a feeling I may never attain. Then, it all began to make sense. I was chasing the wrong thing. The scripture said that God chose me to be a 'prophet', which is "a person regarded as an inspired teacher or proclaimer of the will of God". How could I teach what I had not learned? How can I proclaim his will without being a witness to his work? Understanding that I didn't need to arrive at purpose; but that everything happened for God's purpose changed my life, and it will change yours.

When you look at 'purpose' as your destination, you become preoccupied with creating the fastest route to it. You rush through important lessons in life. You take failures and shortcomings as something pulling you away from your purpose, and it angers you. You develop this fetish for success and become addicted to the chase. You become a goal-chaser relentlessly pursuing that unidentified target until you realize you have hit nothing. I know, because I was you. Being able to make the mental transition from chasing 'purpose' to understanding that I am 'evolving' made it possible for me to release my pain, and it is going to help you, too. The word 'evolve' means to gradually develop over a period into something different and usually more advanced. This means that everything you have experienced from birth to date is part of your evolution into a wiser prophet capable of proclaiming the will of God. Yes, I said it—everything! Even those dark places where you feel cheated, were chosen for you by God for his glory.

In this book, I will walk you from a position of pain to peace to prophecy. As I reflect on key events in my life where I felt cheated until I realized I was chosen, you will see how God chose ordinary people like you and me to be proclaimers of his will. You will see that you and I are no different than Peter, Mary, or David. We are all chosen to be prophets based on how we have experienced his love, protection, peace, grace, forgiveness, miracles, healing power and much more for ourselves. Nothing you have endured is by chance, and you were not cheated; you were CHOSEN for such a time as NOW. So, it's time you reveal those areas where you feel cheated, acknowledge that you are chosen, and step into your role as a prophet of all nations. If you are ready, let's go.

Chapter Two
The Call to Prophesy

On February of 2016, I attended a Prophetic Word Seminar in Birmingham with a group of friends. I had never been to one before, so I was a bit nervous, yet excited. After the opening, we divided into groups. I wasn't with my friends, but I made conversation with the people in my group before it was my turn. There were three prophets in our group—one female and two guys. When it was my turn, I turned on my voice recorder and told them my name. One of the guys opened with prayer and began to speak over me. The female was the last one to speak. Just like the guys, she was on-point in reference to my passion to teach and mentor youth, and my desire to be obedient to God's call on my life. Then, she touched on two words that I really didn't want to hear—past experiences—and proceeded to say that she saw me writing a book.

She said, "Some of the things you need to talk about, you don't really want to, but some people need to hear them so that they can be delivered and encouraged through your sharing." She even acknowledged that I'd heard it before, but I didn't know where to begin and that God wanted me to just open a Word document and start typing. For the next few years, I was constantly reminded about this book, but never opened a Word document.

She was right. I didn't want to talk about some of the mess I had been through. While my professional resume looks stellar—13 years of dedicated and decorated military service, 3 degrees, good credit, community servant, church goer, and much more—I still somehow reduced myself to the motherless, fatherless, divorced, single mother of two children with different daddies who had not arrived to the 'Christian author' status. I had done that with many other opportunities to be influential in the Christian world. I took on small assignments, but I just didn't think I was fully ready, even though I knew exactly what was being spoken into me was already in me. As I began to reflect on my life, most of the opportunities I'd been given were based off prophecy or potential and never my current position or past experiences. I literally had to stop and thank God for the people who saw me before I could even see myself. As the cliché says, 'Favor is not always fair, but it feels good'.

So, what brought the pen to the paper that I am currently writing on as 'my book' because I have no title? Well, I was talking to my friend at the beginning of this year. We both expressed being unfulfilled in 2018 and our desire to do more things of substance in 2019. Even though I felt like I had accomplished a lot academically, professionally, and financially, I somehow ended up spiritually thirsty. Something had to change.

On another occasion, my same friend and I were talking, and she asked, "Have you ever felt like you should write a book?" I responded, "Really, you were there when the woman prophesied to me about writing a book." She was the one who invited me. She had no idea that I had been secretly trying to figure out how I was going to fulfill this prophecy. As I sat down at my kitchen table on New Year's Eve, I wrote 'Complete Rough Draft of Book' as one of my goals for this year. Our connection was confirmation that I had to start writing.

As we continued to talk, the Holy Spirit spoke clearly saying, "The blessing is in the obedience". See, I knew it was not only time; it was urgent. I had been praying and venting about some special circumstances and relationships in my life. As encouraging as my friends were, I am sure they were getting as exhausted as I was. It seemed as if I could accomplish any thing I set my heart and hands on except these little, but BIG things; and you mean to tell me, God was saying that I had to do this to get to that?

I cannot explain the anxiety that came with the thought that God was withholding my request until I released this book. What kind of ransom was that? What book? What would I call it? Who would read it? I had no idea where to start. I had an idea of the things I didn't want to talk about, but that was the point. However, the Holy Spirit said that my blessing is in my obedience. You might be wondering how I know this. Well, I googled it. Yes, you read that last sentence right. I will google anything, and I do this often when trying to understand conversations and signs between me and the Holy Spirit. I don't need a sermon or Bible study to get a word from God. My personal relationship with him allows us to connect in our own special way, so, I typed the phrase 'blessing in obedience' in the search bar of my phone, and it led me to the story about Peter in Luke 5: 1-11.

In the story, Jesus was preaching on the shore of the Sea of Galilee. Peter and another fisherman had docked their boats and were washing their nets. Jesus was on the boat, preaching to the crowd. Afterward, he asked Peter to go out into the deep water and let down his net. Peter explained that they had worked hard all night and caught nothing; however, he ended by saying, "*But if you say so, I'll let the net down again,"* (v. 5); and this time, Peter and his partners' boats were overflowing with fish. Peter was so ashamed, he apologized to Jesus, but, Jesus replied, *"Don't be afraid! From now on you'll be fishing for people!"*

Clearly, it didn't matter how many hours Peter spent out in the water or what was the initial reasoning why he didn't catch any fish. One answer to Jesus' call changed the outcome instantly. This small act of obedience yielded a big blessing. The wonderful thing about being under the grace of God is that it doesn't matter how long you have been trying to do it your own way; the minute you decide to do it his way, your life will change. Two things God reveals through Peter: first, obeying God is never disappointing, and second, obeying God will always bless more than you.

I can imagine how disappointed and exhausted Peter was after being out there all night with nothing to show for it. I can imagine, because I've been Peter in many areas of my life, and you have, too. You try so hard to save and be financially responsible, but those bills keep piling up or an unexpected expense puts you back in the negative. You try so hard to make that relationship work, but it doesn't, and you ended up feeling like you wasted your time. You work overtime with hopes of getting considered for that promotion at work only to get over-looked again.

I remember wanting to be a military recruiter back in 2011. When the Department of the Army selected me, I was ecstatic. I submitted my packet and was ready for school. Long story short, after battling back and forth about the location, my assignment was deleted. They tried giving me several others, but I just felt cheated. I declined to continue my service, and when my time was up, I transitioned into the civilian world.

In 2013, I was teaching Algebra 1 at a high school in Greensboro, Alabama. There was a recruiter, Staff Sergeant Brown, who came to the school regularly. One day, I expressed how I had wanted to be a recruiter and was disgusted when my orders were deleted back in 2011. He suggested that I try again and introduced me to Master Sergeant Benton of the Army National Guard. I explained my goals, and he told me what I needed to do to get an interview. I aced the interview, but there was one issue — I was in the Army Reserves. This was in the spring of 2014 when I initially decided to go get my dream job, and it looked like a long road of possibility and not any promise.

I remember MSG Benton saying, "I can't promise you anything, so I understand if you want to go back to teaching." I didn't go back in August of 2014; I was determined to be a recruiter. The long wait was over in less than 48 hours. I enlisted into the Army National Guard on October 22, 2014, and in-processed into my position as a Full-Time Recruiter in my hometown the next day. What seemed like a possibility for months became my position over night.

To this day, when people ask how I landed my dream job in my hometown, I can only say "It was God." At the appointed time, his will always be fulfilled. Like Peter, I had tried years ago, but it didn't work. The call to prophesy can only be fulfilled at the appointed time once God has prepared you. See, when I tried for the position in 2010 at Fort Campbell, I was in the wrong location, and I wasn't ready. God had to do some more work within me and around me. A lot changed between 2010 and 2014. I experienced some extreme highs and some unthinkable lows, but I learned a lot. The second time around, I didn't have to fight for my position at all. It was as if it was waiting on me; and, I have not been disappointed since but continuously blessed by my obedience.

In Peter's case, he had docked his boat, and Jesus began preaching to the crowd on it. It wasn't until after the sermon that God asked Peter to push the boat out and lower his net. We must stop, listen to God's word and wait for his call before we can proceed to retrieve our blessing or be a blessing to others. Have you been listening to God's word, or are you too busy trying to do things your way? I don't know what happened in the water while Jesus was preaching, but there was a net full of fish waiting for Peter immediately after he obeyed God. Luke 5: 9-10 reads: *"For he was awestruck by the number of fishes they had caught, as were the others with him. His partners, James and John, the sons of Zebedee, were also amazed."* Imagine how the fishermen had felt not catching anything all night. Now, imagine having so much fish that your boat is slowly sinking. Talk about a quick turn of events, and, Peter had nothing different — same fisherman, same sea, same boat, same net, same God. The blessing was in Peter's obedience to God's call, and that one step left he and his friends amazed at the wonderful works of Jesus. Are you tired of being disappointed? Are you ready to be amazed?

The second point in the story of Peter is that obeying God will always bless more than you. Your call is always connected to someone else. Not only were Peter and his partners amazed at the amount of fish they were able to catch; they were chosen to become fishermen of men. In verse 10, Jesus said, *"Don't be afraid! From now on, you'll be fishing for people!"* There was a greater call than feeding the people physically. There was a spiritual hunger that needed to be satisfied, as well.

When the prophet spoke to me about this book, she told me that my testimony wasn't for me, but for someone who needed to hear it. Even though there were things I didn't want to share, knowing that someone's deliverance was tied to my obedience was a call I could not press the reject button on; so, I am writing these words as my obedience to God. Just as Peter's obedience yielded enough fish to make him a fisherman of men and women, I pray that my obedience blesses you and everyone connected to you.

As I reflect on my experiences and whose story has delivered me from my feelings of being cheated, one story comes to mind. I remember one Sunday in the spring of 2016, my pastor preached about being favored in unfavorable circumstances. I have always admired her transparency, but she caught me by surprise when she talked about being pregnant and unmarried in the church many years ago. She talked about the initial embarrassment and how a few women of faith pulled her aside and loved on her despite the circumstances. I had no idea that she had experienced my feelings, and she had no idea I was sitting in my chair pregnant again. Yep, again. I was already divorced with a little girl. I was just coming out of my shell into a woman in the ministry. I was part of JAM (Jesus Acts Ministry) and over the youth praise dance team at church. Being unmarried and pregnant again just felt like a setback, and, because I knew better, I was even more ashamed.

After the church service, I felt so relieved. I was eager to tell my pastor the good news, because she had been where I was at that moment. Her hug and prayer meant more to me than I ever admitted to her. I thank God for the women who poured into her during her time. That hug felt like their love had rested in her soul and was transferred to me that day. Imagine if those ladies had never prepared her for that moment. I am sure those feelings of guilt and shame were hurtful at the time, but they are small compared to the purpose attached to them. To see her walking in her purpose and proclaiming the will of God is exactly what I meant by evolving into purpose. It was in that moment that I realized it was no coincidence that I was in church that Sunday hearing a word of affirmation from someone who had lived through the situation I was in. We were both chosen, and it was my responsibility to take on the torch.

About a month later, I had the opportunity to light my torch during our once-a-month drill with new recruits. I was running with a girl who was late and fussing at her about being slow. Barely able to breathe, she said, "I'm pregnant," and I laughed and said, "Me, too." She quickly replied, "It is not a laughing matter," with a disgusted and defeated look on her face. She explained that she was only a senior in high school, and this was not how she expected to walk across the stage. She went on and on about how her mom was a Christian and was preaching to her. I explained to her that I was a Christian, too, but nowhere near a perfect one and that her situation was no greater sin than mine, being unmarried and pregnant, yet, God loved us both and had a purpose for our lives, and that plan would survive our current circumstances. It's funny looking back on that day. She had no idea; I was just like her, just like I had no idea my pastor had experienced the same thing. Our purpose connects us to people on purpose so that we can proclaim the will of God.

God didn't mistakenly create you. He has a need for you—a purpose that only you can fulfill, a connection that only you can make with certain people. I've never been a science guru, but I remember being taught that no one else has the same DNA. Do you understand that no one has the same spiritual gift as you? In

Jeremiah 1:5, God says, "I chose YOU." Those three words give a clear and profound declaration that ONLY you will experience your life, and only you can fulfill the prophetic mission attached to your purpose. Just think about whose story has helped you heal from a heartbreak, prevented you from making a bad decision, made you feel like you weren't alone in your pain, or motivated you to keep pushing, despite what it looked like. You knew they were placed in your path to meet your need at that time, and it felt good. Imagine where you would be without those people. Now imagine who is missing out on their breakthrough because you have been harboring these feelings of being cheated, instead of understanding that you were chosen for such a time as NOW.

Chapter Three
Chosen Comes with a Choice

When God chose you, he also gave you a choice. John 3: 16 says, "For God so loved the world that he gave his only begotten son, that whosoever believes in him shall not perish but have everlasting life." He didn't say 'everyone', but 'whosoever' believes in him. Salvation is a choice, and so is prophecy. I grew up in an African Methodist Episcopal Church. Every year, we had a revival, and at a certain age, teenagers were expected to sit on what we called the morning bench. This was our transition from being under the umbrella of our parents' salvation to developing our own. They would ask us a series of questions about our beliefs to ensure that we understood what we were doing. Once we gave our lives to Christ and chose him, we were to be baptized. Not like christening, which is the sprinkling we had as babies. This time was the full submersion in the baptism pool. Even though Jesus paid the price long ago and many of us were christened as babies, there comes a time each of us must make a personal commitment to continue to serve God. Just like babies come out of the womb at an appointed time, so must the will of God come out in our lives at an appointed time.

What I love about the word of God is that it always comes with references. You never have to question whether it can be done, because it has already been proven to be true. His word has never come back void. While Jeremiah 1:5 spoke of God choosing you in your mother's womb, it may seem strange, considering what you have endured thus far; but, let's look at the story of Mary. She was an ordinary, Jewish virgin engaged to Joseph. Her résumé read nothing that would have made her deserving of being Jesus' mother. While she may have felt lowly and undeserving in her own eyes and the eyes of those around her, she was valuable in God's eyes. In Luke 1:28-30, the angel identified Mary as the favored one who has found favor with God. It mentions nothing of her being the qualified one. It had nothing to do with who she was, but everything to do with what God wanted to do through her.

Mary was called to the prophetic task of bearing and raising Jesus. Even though God had already chosen Mary, she had to make a choice to answer the call. At the end of her conversation with the Angel, Mary said, "I am the Lord's servant. May it be done to me as you have said." (Luke 1:38) She committed to being used by him, because she believed. While many choose to focus on Mary as the mother of Jesus, there is so much more to be said about her choice. Mary models true discipleship and answering the call to prophesy. She wasn't blessed and favored because she was chosen to birth and raise Jesus. She was favored, because she believed God's word would be fulfilled and made a choice to let it be done through her.

Luke highlights Mary as the willing vessel, not just the virgin woman. Elizabeth was the first confirmation saying, "Blessed is she who believed that there would be a fulfillment of what was spoken by the Lord." Later in Luke 11, Jesus was teaching the crowd and a woman expressed how blessed Mary must be as the one chosen to birth Jesus; he clarifies what is important. He responded, "Blessed rather are those who hear God's word and obey it!" Whew, that should relieve some pressure you have built up inside of you. You may not be a virgin like Mary or engaged to be married to the man of your dreams. Matter of fact, you may be like me — living with one hell of a past, divorced, two different baby daddies, and single. Thank God our credentials aren't in question; our commitment is. Are you willing? Are you available? Do you believe that a miracle of God can be birthed through you? Are you willing to have your business publicized, your past scrutinized, and your future compromised — all for God's glory?

If that's a choice you are willing to make, your life will change! Your past will no longer look or feel painful but more like preparation for prophecy!!! That was for me and you. Let's say it together in present tense, "My past does not look or feel painful. It is my preparation for prophecy!" I am writing these words to you not by chance, but because I have made a choice. The things I didn't want to talk about are easy to release, because I understand that they prepared me for a time such as NOW. I pray that you understand that your reading this is preparing you, as well! Whatever is in you can grow and flow out of you when you become willing. Being a woman didn't make Mary Jesus' mother. There were plenty of other women with a uterus, ovaries and the capabilities to have a baby. Mary was chosen and found favored based on her faith!

Faith was Mary's choice. Because she believed, she was willing to give up her reputation, endure the ridicule and even risk her life in order to fulfill prophecy. She said yes to God's will out of love for him. Mary's willingness to be used by God changed the face of the earth. Don't ever think that you or your call is not as important. What has God called you to do that you have not committed to yet — teaching, dancing, singing, mentoring, praying, or writing? I remember not really understanding why we had to make a commitment. One of my favorite scriptures is Jeremiah 29:11, which says that God knows the plans he has for our lives. If he chose us in our mother's womb and already has the plan outlined, what is the hold-up? See, God isn't going to force you to believe in him, serve him, follow him, or allow him to use you. The call on your life comes with a choice — your choice.

In the story of Mary and Martha, we learn about making a choice to prioritize God. Jesus was a frequent visitor to their house. This visit was nothing special, but the lesson we learn is very critical to our relationship with him. Martha was busy making sure everything was in order. She was cleaning and preparing a big dinner for Jesus while Mary was sitting at Jesus' feet, listening to him talk. In the natural sense, it is understandable that Martha would be irritated and resentful towards Mary. Imagine being busy being a great hostess while your sister sits Indian style, not helping at all. I would have been frustrated, too. Mary was so upset that she approached Jesus and said to him in Luke 10: 40, "Sir, doesn't it seem unfair to you that my sister just sits here while I do all the work? Tell her to come help me." Check out Martha trying to snitch on Mary.

Mary's silence spoke loudly to Jesus. I am here to serve notice that when you choose to prioritize your relationship with God, a lot of people are going to be upset with you. Someone is going to feel like you are ignoring them. Someone is going to feel like you aren't doing enough. Some will simply be jealous, because they feel like they must do more than you are doing to get the same results. Do not respond to the enemy's trick. You cannot compromise your call listening to outside opinions. You must choose to rise above all the noise and worldly pursuits to hear God's voice. Your call to prophesy comes with a responsibility to seek God, learn his word, serve his people and strive to be more and more like him in all that you do.

Like Mary, your love and devotion for being a prophet puts everything else second, even housework. I know you may be looking around and everyone seems to be moving while you are standing still. The feeling of complacency will have you feeling like you need to get up and run, but why run in circles, when you can be still and let God move in you and on your behalf? Take a second and ask, "God, what do you want to do in my life? What do you want me to do with my life?" When you move in obedience to the answers to these questions, God will cover you. Mary didn't have to explain herself to Martha. Jesus defended her and corrected Martha in Luke 10: 41-42, saying, "Martha, dear friend, you are so upset over all these details! There is only one thing worth being concerned about. Mary has discovered it—and I won't take that away from her!" Mary was being obedient and still, even with everything else going on around her. Her stillness was the best move. Being in the presence of Jesus was exactly where she needed to be in that moment.

Are you Mary or Martha in your relationship with God? Are you in the presence of God or roaming around aimlessly in the world? Sometimes we get caught up in the materialistic things of life. Your primary reason for existing is to be a prophet and proclaim God's will through your work. You are called to purposeful living. When you concentrate on your purpose in Christ, everything else will fall in place—your career, your relationship, your finances, your family, and much more. As Martha moved around, she missed the value of being in Jesus' presence. Imagine what you could hear if you were still and available for God to speak to you. Imagine the impact you could have if you open and let God use you. It is like the ringing of a phone. Two things must happen. One, the ringer must be heard. Two, the phone must be answered. Without those two together, no connection can be made.

For years, I've ignored this call. I was Martha — up and moving around. I had a fetish for accomplishments and was addicted to the chase. I was constantly considering changing my career and physical location, adding another degree to my résumé and more. I could accomplish anything except being like Mary — still and focused on what is important — God. What makes it worse is that I've always known that I was called to do something greater than myself. So, I heard the phone ringing, but I chose not to answer it. I can retrace this call all the way back to elementary school.

One year, my aunt had to attend a teacher conference in reference to my behavior. The teacher labeled me as the 'ringleader'. She explained that the other kids were following me, and I was leading them in the wrong direction. I remember saying, "I didn't ask them to follow me." I remember the first few days of basic training like yesterday, even though it was 2005. My drill sergeant called me up to him and said, "You know you can be a great leader, but you have a bad attitude. How do I know that, and I just met you?" I replied, "You are a pretty smart guy, Drill Sergeant." I never really wanted to be a leader, because I was honest enough to know that I wasn't always going in the right direction. Instead of choosing to do right, I preferred not to answer the call.

How many times have you avoided your call because you weren't ready to walk in it? I briefly mentioned the prophet talking about my passion for mentoring teens during the seminar. He was so true. Working in the high schools and working with young recruits during drill, I realized that this wasn't just a career, but a calling. While doing the JAM ministry, I developed this desire to create something similar for young girls. Although I had the idea laid out in my head, I had convinced myself that I wasn't qualified, and no one would value my words. One Sunday in December of 2017, my pastor was talking about the vision for 2018. She brought up Teen Talk — a Bible study call-in that would focus on real-world issues that our youth are having today. As she talked, I heard God say, "That's you." I knew it was for me before she even asked to talk to me after church, yet, it took me some thinking to commit to it.

On the flip side, I would not be where I am professionally had I not answered the call. In the previous section, I acknowledged that every opportunity I've been given was based off my potential and not my position. The last four professional development courses I've attended, I was not the one originally registered for the slot. I was not even the most qualified or at the top of the order of merit. Each time, I received a phone call saying that a slot had become available, along with the question — Will you be ready to go by this date? My immediate response every time was 'yes' with no hesitation or conversation. Imagine if I had said yes to God years ago and fully committed to my call. I've spent years trying to justify my delay while I qualified myself. Reality is, I am no more prepared for this than I was professionally, yet, God saw fit for me to be successful every time. I am ashamed of myself.

With shame comes conviction, and for me, conviction led to commitment. God called Mary to be the mother of Jesus. She made a choice to answer the call. He called me to write this book.

I ran around in circles for years, but now is the time. I have chosen to answer the call; and, he is calling you to fulfill a great purpose. Mary was chosen on purpose. Jesus died on purpose. I am writing this book on purpose. You are reading this on purpose. Someone else's healing, deliverance, and breakthrough is tied to your purpose. Our call comes with a choice to be made. It is your choice, so what will you choose?

Chapter Four
Calling out the Pain

What did I do to deserve this? Why has God allowed me to go through such hard times? Does God not care about me? Am I really saved? Why me? Why my family? How did my life come to this?

How will I get out of this?

While our faith does not exempt us from having these questions, we also must be on guard. Just as we open our mouths to ask these questions of God, and our ears to hear his answers, we open our hearts to Satan's attack. The devil has been waiting on you to question God so that he can intervene and tell you all sorts of lies, hoping you are weak enough to believe them. He knows when you are vulnerable and capitalizes on it. When I reflect on my past experiences, I can see how Satan poured salt on my open wounds with his lies. The top three lies the devil told me:

#1: God took my mother because I was a rebellious teen and took her for granted.

I was one strong-willed, hot-tempered, and rebellious child. I saw my mother cry after parent-teacher conferences because of the way I had behaved. I saw her walk away from me to keep from choking me when I just had to have the last word. I also saw her scrape up her last and borrow money to make sure I got everything I needed and wanted. A few days before she died, I had lost my driver's license. In the process of getting it replaced, we argued, as usual. I made my negligence an emergency for her, as if she didn't have anything else to do. As she shoved my social security card and birth certificate in my hand, she said, "You need to start keeping up with your own stuff. I am not going to be here forever." If I'd known how short our forever would be, I would have taken another approach.

The night before she died, she came to my dance recital rehearsal and was just standing around. I was 17 and too cool to have my mother there with me, so, I rudely rushed her out the building, saying, "I don't need you to stay here with me." If I could have predicted that would be our last night together, I would have been happy for her to stay with me. The devil told me that I didn't deserve her, and God took her away from us to give her the peace she needed. I was mad at me and God.

#2: I was generationally cursed to die at a young age like my parents and grandparents did.

My mother's mother died when my mother was 11 months old. My daddy's mother died when he was 9 years old. At age 17, I was orphaned. When I was younger, I didn't want to have kids, because I felt like I was destined to die before my kids would get grown. I could not imagine leaving them here to be raised by someone else. I didn't want them to feel cheated. This wasn't just a thought in my head. I've had conversations with God about this on several occasions. I've said, "Now listen here, God. You gave me these kids. Don't take me before they are independent and on their own. I want to raise my own kids." As strong as I felt making those statements, I know that they came from a painful and fearful place. How can I believe the devil and try to bargain with God? I could not trust God and believe Satan at the same time. I had a choice to make on whose team I was going to be a member of.

#3: *My past disqualified me for a strong ministry.*

This call has been hunting me down for years. When my friend jokingly says, "Minister Micia," I cringe. When someone makes the statement, "Girl, you are preaching," I cringe. I never wanted to be big in the ministry, because I felt undeserving and incapable of living up to the standard. A few years ago, I met a guy who was interesting, but we lost contact. When we reconnected, he said, "You know, I've been called into ministry." Well, that was it for me. I told my friends, "I can't be nobody's first lady or first anything." It was so funny to them and so serious to me. I was safe staying in my lane, which included praise dancing and youth Bible study at the most.

When I began meditating on this book and God led me to Jeremiah 1:5, the term "prophet" scared me. I just could not fathom me being called a prophet, even though it clearly said that God had already chosen each of us to be a prophet of all nations before we ever knew what the word meant. You should have seen me scrolling through my phone, reading different versions of the same verse. Now that was a strong word for a lowly woman like me, and, you want me to write about prophecy in my first book. Really, God?

These are the top three lies the devil told me. Yes, I was weak enough to believe each one for years. These lies played an influential role in my life. They have affected my relationships, my career, my goals, and my mindset. I felt bitter and secretly guilty about my mother's death for years. When I was a young adult, my biggest fear was being unsuccessful. After having kids, dying before they are grown has risen to the top of my list. I still shy away from being strong in the ministry, because I don't feel worthy of a large platform. I have done and thought some things I am ashamed of because of what I believed to be true. They say you can't heal what you won't reveal. These are my truths. What has the devil told you about your past experiences and future possibilities that have you feeling cheated and unworthy?

As you understand and answer the call on your life, you must call out those areas where you feel cheated. If not, the pain will lie dormant and attack you when you are not prepared. It is like the devil has a GPS tracker on you. As soon as you begin to run toward destiny, he delivers a stunning blow. Sometimes it's a friendly reminder of a painful experience. Other times, it's a highlighter placed on your current status. Either way, it leaves you feeling heavy. How do I know? It happens to me. It has been happening since I was a young kid. I can go all the way back to elementary school.

I know we are just getting to this section of the book, but this was the first step in the writing process for me. When the prophet spoke of the book and the things I didn't want to write about, she was talking about the pain. I knew that I had to come to terms with what I needed to release before I could expect the spirit to come through with the content of this book. So, I sat in my room in silence and poured all my pain out on a piece of paper. I cried crocodile tears. I got angry. I laughed at myself. Most of all, I released the pain that had been lying dormant in my heart and in my mind. I had to own these feelings, because they owned me. At times, they consumed my thoughts, overshadowed my accomplishments, and diminished my dreams. This is what I had to call out.

#1: The fatherless girl

I was in the fourth grade at Valley Grande Elementary School, on the playground with my best friends. Tiffany's dad had just died in an accident. Jennifer and I had already lost our dad at a young age. Ashley said, "I guess I am the only one with a daddy now." While we were just kids and that was an honest assessment, those words stung that day, and even writing them today hurts my heart. I was 18 months old when my father was killed. I have a few pictures and lots of memories from family and friends, but growing up, I felt cheated. I never attended a father-daughter dance, I never heard the words, "… escorted by her father" on Senior Night, and I will never hear him say, "I do," when asked who gives this woman to be married on my wedding day. I felt cheated. I used to wonder why God took my dad away from me at such an early age. Did he not understand how much I needed him?

I spent much of my childhood wondering what my daddy talked, looked, and acted like. While family can tell you stories and show you pictures, there is a void they cannot fill. It's an awkward feeling to be in the grocery store and someone says, "Ewe, you look just like Scoop." It is hard to get the picture when you're missing half of the portrait. As I got older, this void and lack of experience bled into my relationships. Having kids reminded me that they don't have a Papa, so the cheated feeling transfers to them. I remember when a fellow soldier was killed in Afghanistan. He was a father of five children, with the youngest one being an 11-year-old girl. As I looked at her during the funeral and burial, my heart broke into a million pieces, knowing that she would experience those same feelings of being cheated out of her daddy. I could not stop the tears from falling. I don't remember my daddy's funeral, but I felt like I was there watching that little girl bury her daddy that day. I felt cheated.

#2: He took my mama, too

I remember the day my mother died. My grandfather had suffered a stroke and was in ICU. My mother was headed to pick up his wife to take her to visit him. It was rainy, and the roads were wet. Her car collided with that of an elderly lady. When we received the call, my stepfather and I rushed to the scene of the accident, not knowing whether she was dead or alive. All we knew was she was in an accident, and they could not get her out of the car. When I got there, I knew it was over. I will never forget that white sheet and the coroner's car. I laid out in the middle of the road and cried out to God, "What are we supposed to do without a momma? I already don't have a daddy."

To make matters worse, my brother was on the other side of the accident and one of the first responders to the scene. I remember my mother saying, "If something ever happens to me, take care of my baby." He was her baby. I felt for him. He was cheated, too. For so many years, I was angry, because I felt we were cheated. As if losing one parent wasn't enough, I was left motherless and fatherless at the age of 17. Not to mention, the elderly lady survived with minor bruises, the accident was reported my mother's fault, and we experienced major financial issues with the funeral expenses. Talk about the ultimate feeling of being cheated. My senior year was rough. I cried for homecoming, prom, and graduation. Even with all my achievements and great memories, I felt cheated.

#3: I'm 0-2 in the relationship department

I remember being in an unhealthy relationship and fighting not to get divorced and become a statistic. Seemed like the more I fought internally, the more the devil showed up physically. I thought I had done it the right way — career, marriage, and a child. Only to end up in the reverse — the child, failed marriage, and unfulfilling career. Reality was, it was not God-ordained, and it was mentally draining. When I finally left, Honey was 11 months old, and we stayed in my auntie's house for a few months. The tears I cried holding my sweet baby who had no understanding of the hell going on around her. How badly I wanted to give my daughter the life I never had. We didn't even make it to her first birthday. One thing I hated was not having a baby picture of me with my mom and dad. I remember having to copy and paste one for our first anniversary dinner, and now, my daughter didn't have one either. This time, I not only felt cheated, I felt like my daughter was cheated. As a mom, the feeling of failing hurt worse than all the pain I had endured.

So, how did I end up with a second child and single? Same script, different cast, except this time, I didn't go through with the wedding. With save-the-dates in my laundry room and a dress in my son's closet, I had to make an honest and healthy decision. Not only did I lose money, but my daughter lost her second daddy, and my son lost the chance to grow up with his daddy in the house. Even knowing that it was the best decision for us as a couple, knowing that my kids would be affected by this long after I got over it was shattering. It was also convicting. See, I was always taught that when you know better, you do better. This wasn't my first rodeo, and I knew better, but I didn't do better. I went back and tried to make it work and failed. I felt better, knowing I had given it my all, but I still felt like my kids were cheated. My whole goal was to give them what I never had, and I had failed twice.

#4: He took my niece, too

I was sitting at home on New Year's Eve 2014 when I received a phone call from my brother. He always says the most serious things in a joking way, so, I knew when he said, "How about this?" It was either serious or seriously funny. Well, he went on to tell me that a DNA test had been done, and my niece was not his child. You did what? It said what? She is what? But wait—she looks like me. She has our last name. I can see my mother in her eyes. She has been in our family since birth. What do you mean she doesn't belong to us? I was heartbroken, angry, confused. I questioned God. I questioned the motive of the test, the validity of the test, and what should be done with the results. I even wished I didn't even know. I wanted no part of this disaster. How could someone clip the wings of my earthly angel just like that? As cheated as I felt, my heart broke for this eight-year-old child whose identity just changed. I had survived being fatherless, motherless, and much more in life, but I never wanted her to have to feel as lost and cheated as I'd felt. Reality was—she was now part of the "cheated", crew and I could not protect her forever.

#5: The successful statistic

I remember sitting on the hiring board for work. I had never sat on one before, so I was so proud to be chosen to assist with selecting the future of our organization. I was the youngest person and the only female. This was during the spring of 2016 when there had been a spree of mass school shooting across the country. Between interviews, one of the guys broke the news of the shooting at a high school in Maryland. As we expressed our sympathy and frustration alike, my commander said, "You know what is eating away at America from the inside out? These broken homes! Single mothers raising boys with no men in the home." I don't remember much more of the conversation, but I remember the feeling like it was yesterday. In the room full of married men, I sat there as a single mother of two kids who had been raised by a single mom of two kids. I was the 'issue'. I am not sure whether my brown skin turned red or if I slid under the table to hide my face, but I know my heart took a nice stab that day. I not only felt cheated, but I felt like a cheater, too.

An old English proverb says "forewarned is forearmed." This means that if you know of possible danger before it happens, you can be better prepared to deal with it. By now, you should be at a point where you can boldly call out your pain. It has been calling you out all these years, so, it is about time that you issue some payback. Grab a piece of paper, and get in a comfortable space. Write down five things that make you feel unworthy of being a prophet. Here are the first five things that come to my mind:

1. Not growing up in a two-parent household
2. Getting divorced
3. Having a bad reputation from past behavior
4. Having a second child out of wedlock
5. Clubbing and drinking

Understanding and answering the call was an emotional high for me. I was pumped up and ready to take on the world. Calling out the pain felt like a 100-foot plunge into the depths of my heart with no cushion. I wanted to just write enough to get through it, but God kept saying to go back and flush those feelings out. When I wanted to just move forward and make peace with the process, he kept telling me, "Go back and make peace with your pain." I was getting frustrated, but I had to keep telling myself it was necessary. Have your flushed out all your feelings? Have you touched those areas that you worked so hard to bury and vowed never to dig them up again? Don't be like me. I wanted to just write down 1-5 and move on. In my head, I was like a little kid saying, "There you have it. I said it. Now, let's move on."

I am here to tell you that saying it is only the beginning. I challenge you to use all your senses when calling out the pain that has been holding you hostage. See yourself in that moment. Feel how you felt way back then and when you talk about it now. Hear those words spoken to you that made you feel so low and unworthy. Taste that bitterness and resentment you bite into every time you are reminded of that person who broke your heart, your trust, and stole your smile for a while. It may sound crazy, and you may feel crazy, but when you allow yourself to touch on every area of your life that the devil has occupied, you take away his power. See, he wants you to leave some for him to come back and feed on later.

I watch a lot of HGTV. My favorite show is "Fixer Upper" with Chip and Joanna. When a family finally chooses a house, they get right on the job. Chip's favorite day is Demolition Day. While Joanna creates a vision of the family's dream home, he is having the time of his life ripping the house apart. Sounds like an easy transition until something comes up, like termites or asbestos. Termite damage is visible during an initial inspection or demolition; however, the asbestos is not. Instead, samples of suspected asbestos fibers are sent to a professional laboratory to be tested. Asbestos cannot be seen with the naked eye. At the point where either of these are found, all construction comes to a halt until these are cleared.

The transition from pain to peace to prophecy is much like watching "Fixer Upper". There is some pain in your life that is like the termites. It is visible to you, your circle of family and friends, and the enemy. They witnessed you endure the loss of a loved one, a miscarriage, divorce, financial difficulties, sickness and other visible drama like these. On the flip side, there is some pain that is like asbestos, hidden and not easily detected with the natural eye. This is the depression that you hide so well within your daily routine. This is the infertility that no one knows is the reason why you don't have kids yet. It's the guilt from the abortion no one knew you had. It's the shame you masked under that strong, confident presence. It's the fear that prevents you from chasing your dreams. This type of pain is the easiest to hide, but the hardest to call out. Recognizing the type of pain you are experiencing is critical to developing a plan of attack to call it out and deactivate its power and influence in your life.

Chapter Five
Making Peace with the Process

A s I coach myself through this journey from pain to peace to prophecy, I am reminded of the last time I rode a rollercoaster. It was about four months ago. I went to Sea World in San Antonio, Texas, with my cousins. I love amusement parks and heights. I was like a little kid running around looking for the next thrill. We kept jumping in line to ride as many times as possible before it was time to go. My favorite ride, no matter where I am, is the one with the biggest dips, jerks, and turns. I am all for the highs. I also understand that the lows are equally important.

I would not get the thrill of a rollercoaster if it were all about the highs. This journey is very much like a rollercoaster ride, so, enjoy the highs, lows, and curves with the understanding that they make the ride worthwhile. Once you drop down and dig up all those painful experiences and circumstances that have made you feel cheated, it is not over. You can't stay in that valley. Making peace with the process is the next step and the uphill journey from pain to prophecy.

As I mentioned earlier, the best thing about the word of God is that it comes with verifiable references. These references add valuable insight to our lives. Honestly, I'm not interested in reading the Bible from start to finish. I'm a more intentional reader. I like to read what is relevant to my life and my journey, so that I can be mentally prepared to weather any storm that arises. In the next few pages, we are going to look at the lives of four of our biblical siblings. I don't like to use the term- characters. It just seems so fictitious. If we are truly going to be God's children, we must acknowledge our biblical family, so, we are going to discuss the journey from pain to peace to prophecy of our four cousins: Esther, Joseph, the blind man, and the woman with the issue of blood.

Esther: From Orphan to Opportunity

I was told that I was the Esther of my family on a few occasions in the past. Several people have prayed for me and brought up Esther. It didn't mean much to me. I am not a Bible guru, so I never put much thought into it. I know four things about Esther.

1. Esther was an orphan who was raised by her cousin.
2. She was Jewish, an unfavorable blood line.
3. She went through a purification process.
4. She saved her people.

This is what I know about me. I was an orphan raised by my auntie for much of my life. I have a not-so-favorable background. I'm not all pure, but I am a long way away from my old self, as far as my attitude and actions. So, I would say that I am in the purification process. I'd like to save people—not in a medical sense but in a mental and spiritual sense, so, I could relate to Esther on the surface. When I really began to study her story, I was amazed at her journey from orphan to opportunity.

Esther had experienced the pain of being an orphan. Both of her parents died, and she was raised by her cousin, Mordecai. I can imagine the feeling of abandonment she masked beneath all the beauty she effortlessly projected outward. I have experienced it first-hand. A lot of people think that abandonment feelings only come from being intentionally left. See, Esther's parents and my parents didn't leave us; they died. I understand that now, but to a child who only knows one thing — that children are supposed to have two parents — it feels like abandonment. We learn so much from our parents, and much of our initial identity and knowledge comes from what we experience through them. To be robbed of this experience, makes you feel cheated.

To make matters worse, before she could even find her own identity, Esther was given one. Her cousin, Mordecai, sent her to the palace to compete to be the queen. The king instantly admired her and chose her over all the other women. Just reading this part makes the story seem like a fairy tale, whereas the common girl would have been overjoyed being chosen by the prince. Well, not in this case. Esther didn't want to be a queen. In fact, she did nothing to stand out and hoped that she didn't get picked, yet, the king delighted in her and chose her. She was forced into a marriage with a man she didn't know. To add to the pain, she was told to hide her nationality and family background. This is another level of abandonment.

Let's stop right here and make peace with the issue of abandonment. On the outside, it looked like Esther had been chosen to be the queen for all the glitz and glamour. We can make an educated guess that the other girls were disappointed and jealous at the favor that Esther had no desire for but received anyway. Do you feel like Esther? Have you been in some places and positions that seemed like the golden opportunity to those looking in from the outside? Yet you were miserable, hurting, and hiding who you really were inside? You've gone to bed restless, and if you are a secret cry-baby like me, you've soaked up pillows with tears at night. The thought of going back to those places makes you cringe. If you're still in that place, getting out of there is a dream.

Now, take a deep breath, and let this sink in. God hid Esther in the palace so that she could get in position for her purpose. God placed Esther on the throne even before the Jews faced the possibility of complete destruction so that when trouble came, a person of value to the King would already be in the position to help the people. He already knew what was going to unfold. When I read this story a couple years ago, I read it with the understanding that the purification process was for Esther's queenship. Now, I see the purification process was tied to a purpose so much greater than her. She had to get rid of shyness and feelings of abandonment that had come to the palace with her so that she could become the BOLD woman of God willing to approach the king to save the Jewish people. Let's look at how the plot unfolds.

In the story, Mordecai overheard the guards plotting to as-sassinate King Xerxes, so he warned Esther. In turn, she let her husband know so that he could protect himself. The king had the guards hanged and gave credit to Mordecai for alarming him. Then, he gave Haman, the Agagite, the highest place of honor above the other nobles in the palace. Everyone knelt and paid honor to him except Mordecai. There had been a long feud between the Agagites and the Jews, so Mordecai had no respect for Haman. The lack of respect made Haman furious, but after learning that Mordecai was a Jew, he was enraged. He decided not only to kill Mordecai but made plans to destroy all the Jews throughout the kingdom of Xerxes.

Mordecai was devastated and sent word to Esther, asking her to go before the king and plead for the safety of her people. There was one issue with his request. Esther had not been summoned to the king in over 30 days, and anyone who reported to the king without being summoned would be put to death unless the king chose to spare their life. Esther's response was not what he wanted to hear, but it was the law of the kingdom. Mordecai's response to her was rather brutal, to me. He said, "Do you think because you are in the king's house you alone of all the Jews would escape?" Had he forgotten that he was the one who instructed her to hide her identity? Now, he was throwing it in her face. Thank God we already made peace with the issue of abandonment, because I was about to check Mordecai. It's not about his response, but her responsibility. He wasn't calling her out; it was time for her to come out.

Esther had a choice to make. She could play it safe and protect one person—herself—or, she could risk her own life for the possibility of saving her family and her people. During the process from her pain of abandonment to the peace in the palace to her opportunity to save her people, Esther was unsure of her purpose. Mordecai, who sent her to the palace, wasn't even sure of Esther's purpose. In Esther 4:14, Mordecai says, "If your keep quiet at a time like this, deliverance and relief for the Jews will arise from some other place, but you and your relatives will die. **Who knows if perhaps you were made Queen for just such a time as now**?" Neither of them knew if, how or why God was using Esther.

Esther could have chosen to continue to live hidden but comfortable on her throne of security in the palace. The king didn't know she was Jewish, and unless Mordecai told him, her secret would survive the death of the Jews. If she speaks up now, her secret will be revealed, and, who knows what will happen? Maybe the king will save his queen alone, or, maybe he will put her out of the palace and destroy her, along with her people, or, he could grant favor upon the Jews because of Esther's bold leap of faith. Even with all the uncertainties and possible danger, she chose to be two things: humble and obedient.

Esther didn't know what the outcome would be, but she made peace with the fact that she could not stay silent. Esther was humble enough to know two things. First, she had to be the one to do it. Second, she could not do it alone. She made peace with the fact that her hidden identity would be the one thing that would give King Xerxes compassion for the Jewish people. She made peace with the pain of being an orphan as she knew she had the opportunity to save her people. She could not sit quietly and enjoy her queenship at the cost of the lives of the Jewish people. Her secret nationality became her success strategy. She used what I'd like to call the three Ps to purpose—pause, prepare, and power.

She PAUSED to reflect on what was important to her, her role, and her responsibility. Although she wasn't sure what the outcome would be, she knew she had to press forward. She knew she could not do it alone, so she called on the Jewish people. She PREPARED by asking Mordecai, the people of Suna, and the attendants, to fast with her. She asked that they not eat or drink anything at all for three days. Afterward, she was going to the king and in her words, "If I perish, I perish." So, Esther put on her robe and went to see her husband. He asked her what she wanted and offered her anything, even up to half of the kingdom. Before she could even get her request out, it was granted. Whew, there is a special kind of POWER in the favor of God. Power that can do more than you could imagine or ask for. Watch this.

Esther requested that the king and Haman attend a banquet. The night before the banquet, the king could not sleep. He realized that he had not thanked Mordecai for saving his life. While the king was thinking, Haman was outside the court, planning the death of Mordecai. He had a pole set up and planned to ask the king to have Mordecai hung on it. The king recognized Haman was outside and called for him. He asked Haman what should be done for someone whom the king wanted to honor. Haman thought he could only be talking about him and suggested that the man be given a royal robe and led through the city streets on a special horse, proclaiming his honor. The king ordered Haman to get the robe and horse and do just that for Mordecai; and, he did it with shame in his heart.

At the banquet, again, the king asked Esther what she wanted and offered her anything, including up to half of the kingdom. She answered, "If I have found favor with you, Your Majesty, and if it pleases you, grant me my life — this is my petition — and spare my people — this is my request — for I and my people have been sold to be destroyed, killed and annihilated." The king only asked her two questions — Who is he, and where is he who dared to do such a thing? When she told him it was Haman, the king was enraged. Haman was ashamed and begged Esther to pardon him. In the end, Haman was killed and hung on the same pole he had set up for Mordecai.

Esther's step of faith activated the power that was already in her. The king cared nothing about her secret nationality, and, Haman's plot to kill Mordecai backfired on him. Not only were Esther and Mordecai safe; the King revoked Haman's plan to destroy the Jews and granted them safety forever. The power of favor took her from being unsure to being insured forever. She just wanted to be safe from Haman's plot. Now, there will never be another plot against her people. Because she was Jewish and the king found favor in her, he extended the favor to everyone connected to her.

What are some issues you have gotten used to dealing with? What are some desires you have inside that you have gotten used to not seeing on the outside? I'm not calling you, but remember, when you come out, everything inside that didn't get called out is coming out with you. You may be comfortable with your impurities and don't mind living with the imperfections. After all, we aren't designed to be perfect, but when you know that becoming the best version of you is tied to someone else, it is a different type of call. Like Esther, your purpose is greater than you. God has something buried inside of you that can change your life, your family's future, and the lives of many others for generations to come.

Are you ready for the 3 Ps? Can you pause and ask God, "What is it that you would have me to do with my life?" Are you willing to be still long enough to listen to his response? Part of making peace with the process is preparing a peaceful environment for you to grow in. The power cannot be activated without preparation. Do you have a circle willing to fast and pray on your behalf? Support goes a long way on the journey from pain to peace to prophecy.

I know there is this cliché that says we should move in silence, and, as I proceeded to write this book, I was skeptical about telling people my plans. I started telling certain people — my inner circle of friends, my close family, my pastors, and prayer partners. The prayers, resources, support and love they have provided through this journey have been essential to me completing what you are reading now. There were times I needed just a few hours to myself to write and God sent someone to get my kids. There were places I was stuck in the writing process and God sent the next paragraph in a random conversation. These interactions were able to occur because I was connected to the right people at the right time for the right purpose.

Check out this bonus. As I was researching Esther, I realized that God is not mentioned in the book of Esther at all. It never talks about God doing anything, yet we can see his power throughout the book, from Esther transitioning from an orphan to a queen, to Mordecai saving King Xerxes, to King Xerxes saving Mordecai from Haman's death plot. From a plot to destroy the Jews to a decree saving and securing the entire Jewish race, God was working his power behind the scenes through special people at a specific time. WOW! That is a word itself. I just felt an amazing sense of peace come over me. When you know whose you are, you never have to question where you are and if he is with you.

In Deuteronomy 31:8, Moses tells Joshua, "Do not be afraid or discouraged, for the Lord will personally go ahead of you. He will be with you; he will neither fail you nor abandon you." Even when you may not be able to feel his presence, you can make peace with the process, knowing that he has already gone before you and laid out a path to success. His desires for you will be fulfilled. He has never failed.

Joseph: From Prisoner to Prince

Imagine having dreams of being a ruler and ending up enslaved and jailed for a crime you didn't commit. Does not sound "dreamy" but more like a bad dream or a not-so-funny joke. Well, it is a true story. It happened to Joseph. I remember the first time God spoke to me through the story of Joseph. My cousins and I were in San Antonio , Texas, for a basic training graduation. That Sunday, we had the opportunity to attend church with all of the trainees and visiting families. The pastor spoke on the importance of favor and forgiveness. The word was so good, I still have the notes in my phone. I even went back to read the scripture to add to them. I got so much, I had to break it down in sections.

First, who was Joseph? Joseph was the 11th son of Jacob and labeled the 'chosen one' by his brothers. Jacob openly expressed his love for Joseph. His brothers viewed him as the tattle tale who always took bad reports to their father. Because of his favor and actions, they resented him. To make matters worse, Joseph started telling his brothers about these prophetic dreams. In his dreams, Joseph was ruling over his family! Imagine this, the tattle tale, favorite child is now the future ruler.

Second, what happened to Joseph? The animosity grew so much that the brothers plotted to kill Joseph in the wilderness. Reuben, the oldest brother, objected to killing him, so they decided to sell Joseph into slavery. They fooled their father into believing he had been slain by a wild beast! Joseph was sold to a high-ranking Egyptian official named Potiphar. This is where the plot shift comes into play. Yes, his body was sold into slavery, but his mind was free. Joseph excelled at his duties and eventually became one of Potiphar's most trusted servants. Joseph had divine favor everywhere, and everyone connected to him was blessed. Potiphar felt this and placed Joseph over everything he had. Joseph had gone from the chosen son to the chosen slave.

While Joseph found favor with Potiphar, his wife was developing an interest in Joseph. She asked him to sleep with her, but he refused to. He respected not only his master, but also God. She would not accept no for an answer, so, she caught him off-guard one day and grabbed him by the coat. Joseph slid out of his coat and ran. She used his coat to frame him for trying to sleep with her, as if she was the one who refused him. When Potiphar found out, he put Joseph in jail. Pharaoh, the warden, took a special liking to Joseph—so much so, that he placed him in control of all prison personnel and operations. Now, Joseph had gone from the chosen slave to the chosen prisoner.

In prison, Joseph met the cupbearer and the baker. One night, they both had dreams that saddened them, because they could not understand them. Joseph saw their sadness and asked them what was wrong. He explained the meaning of each of their dreams. The cupbearer was to be released from prison and restored to his old position. The baker was to be killed. Both of those interpretations came true.

Two years later, Pharaoh had two dreams that left him confused and disturbed. He traveled all over Egypt to every magician and wise man, but no one could interpret it. The chief baker remembered when Joseph interpreted his dream and suggested that Pharaoh find Joseph, so, Pharaoh sent for Joseph and asked if he could interpret his dreams. Joseph replied, "Not by me, but God will give Pharaoh a good answer."

Pharaoh explained his dreams, and Joseph explained their meanings. The dreams were connected. They were God's way of revealing what was to come to the land of Egypt—seven years of plenty of food followed by seven years of famine. The years of famine would deplete the resources, and the people of Egypt would be destroyed. Joseph outlined a plan to store up food during the years of plenty to feed the people during the years of famine. He also suggested that Pharaoh find a man who was understandable and wise to carry out his plan.

Pharaoh and his servants were pleased with the plans. He asked them, "Can we find a man like this who has in him the spirit of God?" Then, he looked at Joseph and explained that no one was more qualified than him. After all, God had given the interpretation of the dream and the plan to Joseph; so, Pharaoh put Joseph in charge of all the land of Egypt and made him second ruler. He gave him a ring and a wife. Now, Joseph had gone from the "chosen prisoner" to the "chosen ruler".

Joseph went on to fulfill his plan. He stored up so much food, he lost track. When the years of famine came, he had a plan and plenty of food. When times worsen , people came to see him to buy food. Just like everyone else, there came a time when Jacob, Joseph's father, was low on food, so, he sent his sons to Egypt for food. When they arrived, they bowed down and asked Joseph for food. While he immediately knew who they were, they didn't recognize him, so Joseph played it off.

Joseph questioned his brothers about their father and tested their obedience and loyalty. Eventually, he broke down and told them who he was. They were speechless and ashamed. They begged his forgiveness. In Genesis 45: 5, 7-8, Joseph settled the score once and for all. He said, "But don't be upset, don't be angry with yourselves for selling me to this place. It was God who sent me here ahead of you to preserve your lives. God sent me ahead of you to keep you and your families alive and to preserve many survivors. So, it was God who sent me here, not you! And he is the one who made me an advisor to Pharaoh — manager of his entire palace and the governor of all Egypt." Joseph had his brothers go back and get their father and entire family to live near him so that he could take care of them.

It had been over 20 years between the dreams and the manifestation, yet, Joseph never lost sight of who he was and whose he was. He never lost faith in his dreams, and God never left his side. When asked to interpret Pharaoh's dreams, he acknowledged God as the giver of the interpretations. Habakkuk 2:3 reads, "For the revelation awaits an appointed time; it speaks of the end and will not prove false. Though it lingers, wait for it; it will certainly come and will not delay." This scripture reminds me of the lyrics of a song I often sing—' He who has begun a great work in you is faithful to perform it.' Just because God doesn't rescue you immediately doesn't mean he has abandoned you. Trust the process!

I can imagine the feelings Joseph could have harbored as he interpreted others' dreams that manifested in the earthly realm while his lingered in his head. I wonder if he went to sleep, wondering if his time would come. I wonder if he felt cheated or like he was dealt the wrong fate. I can hear Joseph questioning God a little like this—Really? You just want me to keep interpreting and watching dreams come true while you have yet to fulfill your promise to me?" Even if Joseph felt these feelings, he trusted the process from the field to slavery, from slavery to the prison, and from the prison to the palace. He didn't search for favor everywhere he went; favor found him. He did nothing extraordinary to set himself apart, except be obedient in the position he was in.

As I write this story to you at this point in my life, I understand the importance of having the right perspective. This story can be spun two ways. I could look at it as the devil attacked Joseph because he saw the call on his life. The devil could be to blame for Joseph's ruined relationship with his father and his time as a slave and prisoner. I could give the devil credit for Joseph's trials, just as I had given him credit for many of the struggles I experienced in life. Or, God could be given the credit for orchestrating the slavery and imprisonment to strengthen him. Joseph's journey tells the story of strength being built in two key areas of life—faith and forgiveness.

Joseph never mentioned his dreams to anyone else other than his brothers. Even as he was interpreting dreams that came true in front of him, he never brought up his—not even to his brothers once they were reunited; yet, it was evident that he held them in his heart, because he knew exactly who had "set him apart" to save his family. When in a position to call his brothers out on their plot to destroy him, he used three powerful words: "It was GOD!" He didn't take credit for the revelations given to him about Pharaoh's dreams, and he didn't give his brothers credit for his position. He knew who had been working in his favor the whole time. He had carried those childhood dreams for over 20 years in silent faith until they became spoken facts.

Whew, that just touched my soul. Do you have Joseph's level of faith and forgiveness, or have you forgotten about the dreams God promised you? See, I have a few things that I'm trusting God to deliver when it comes to my family. I'm not afraid to admit that my faith waivers, depending on my situation. I have never been a slave or prisoner like Joseph, but my faith has been a captive to negative thoughts—thoughts like, It won't happen for me. My desires do not exist. It is too late for me. I could go on and on. Don't be like me. Be like Joseph, because that is my goal.

Forgiveness set Joseph's family and many generations free, but it also freed him to be used by God! The other person may not deserve it, but who are we talking about freeing—you or them? It is not about the pain the situation caused you. It is about the promise and the peace you get to carry for the rest of your life. When God can use you, you can fulfill the prophecy assigned to your life. Hidden in the offense is the opportunity to be who God called you to be. Your life doesn't have to look anything like your dreams right now to be right in God's perfect plan.

Joseph was chosen out of eleven brothers to save his family and change the tradition of his bloodline for generations to come. Did you catch that? If not, let me bring it home. You are not the black sheep of your family; you are the chosen one. They didn't abandon you. God separated you to reposition you. Joseph was on the path to his purpose. Yes, it included betrayal by his brothers, being sold into slavery, false accusations, and imprisonment. It all seems unfair, just like many of the things you and I have experienced, but look where he ended up—second ruler to Pharaoh and reunited with his family. The only thing Joseph had to do in the process was be obedient and patient. It's time you do the same.

The dream you had, the affirmation you speak over yourself daily, and the words spoken over your life will not be destroyed, no matter how many delays and detours you encounter. God's word will never return void. You will be victorious. There is no situation that God is not able to use for his good. Even when we find ourselves in distressing circumstances that may be unjust, just as they were in Joseph's life, we must remain faithful and accept that God is ultimately in charge. If we do these things, we can be confident that God will reward our faithfulness in time. It may be suddenly for some and slowly for others, but surely, he will ALWAYS come through for his children.

From Issue to Insured

I became familiar with the parable of the woman with the issue of blood in 2009. This was before I really began reading my Bible on my own. But I loved praise dancing. I was looking for a song to teach the youth at church, and I ran across a song titled, "One Touch", by Nicole C. Mullen. The song just captured my spirit and took me to a place of worship and peace. I've been at some low points in life where I felt like the woman with the issue — all cried out. I'm not ashamed to admit that some of my lowest points have produced my greatest praise. At those points, I knew that if God didn't step in, I was going to lose my mind. The story of the woman with the issue and the song remind me that God has the power to change my situation as instantaneously as the blood dried up when the woman touched the hem of his garment. Before I break into a praise dance, let's look at the woman.

Three things to be noted about the unnamed woman: One, she had a bleeding condition that had lasted for 12 years. Two, she had spent all her money seeking medical intervention, but she was only left in a worsened condition. Three, she was deemed ceremonially unclean in the Jewish culture. This meant that she was banned from the public, and anything that she touched would become unclean, too. Can you imagine living with such a condition? Not being able to enjoy life freely. Ostracized and restricted to certain places.

Esther was a queen with automatic favor. Joseph was destined from a boy to be great. Now, we have the woman with the issue.

She didn't even have a name. She had been isolated and deemed unclean. She wasn't even supposed to be in the building, but she was desperate!!! Desperation will cause you to be deliberate in getting to your deliverance! Have you ever been desperate for something from God? Did you make your way to his presence, or just pray and wait? Jesus was on the way to heal someone else when he stopped by the temple. The woman made her way to him!

She made peace with the fact that man could not do it, and she could not wait. She had made up her mind that she was going to make a change and do whatever was necessary to get that touch. Though her body was physically sick, she was psychologically healthy enough to know that her healing would be spiritual, so, when she heard Jesus was in the temple... she deliberately made her way to the temple and through the crowd! The scripture says, "For she thought to herself, 'If I can just touch his robe, I will be healed.'" (Mark 5:28) She was called into action by a single thought. No one had done it before her or told her it would work. She was desperate and determined to get to the feet of Jesus.

I love how the songwriter puts it — "If I could just press my way through this madness..." The crowd in the Bible symbolizes the madness in the world and in our hearts that often blocks us from fully receiving God in our lives. If you can just focus on starting your business, writing your book, eating healthy, exercising daily, restoring that broken relationship, or whatever else it may be. If you can just FOCUS; get you some tunnel vision, so you can see your vision all the way through. When you understand that some issues flowing through your body, your home, your family are just a "you and God" thing—you are going to have to stop making these arrangements and alterations to fit the crowd and adjust your vision to focus only on him.

The story of the woman with the issue is   in three books of the Bible — Matthew, Mark, and Luke. I love reading all three accounts of the story, because it blesses my soul differently in each one. There are two things to be noted about Jesus' response to the woman's touch. Luke 8:46 reads, "But Jesus said, 'Someone deliberately touched me, for I felt healing power go out from me.'" The use of the word 'deliberately' shows just how intentional the woman was.

When Jesus asked the disciples who touched him, they blew him off. The place was crowded, and there were too many people to tell who could have bumped into Jesus. However, it was not the mistaken bump or unintended touch in passing. Jesus knew that it was intentional and powerful enough to draw power from him. There are some blessings and breakthroughs we won't be able to stumble across or simply bump into. We are going to have to be intentional about the way we move and who we move toward. In the midst of the crowd the woman set her eyes on Jesus and moved toward him — deliberately.

The second note is Jesus' response to the woman. After she broke down and told him what she had done, he said to her, "Daughter, your faith has made you well. Go in peace. Your suffering is over" (Mark 5:34). Whew, what a shift. She went from being the unnamed woman to being called daughter by Jesus--all because of her faith. Jesus didn't seek the woman with the issue; she sought him. Her faith was the key element in the process from pain to peace to prophecy. This story solidified the meaning of the phrase, ' Put some feet to your faith'. She put feet to her faith and was rewarded her healing. Imagine being labeled an issue most of your life. Now, boom. After one touch that you technically stole, you are now being called 'daughter' by Jesus.

Not only did that touch put an expiration date on her issue, but it put an end to her isolation.

The beautiful thing about the woman with the issue of blood is that she could have spent the rest of her life with that same issue. She had been conditioned to live with it. She knew where she was supposed to go. She knew how to manage her issue, but she knew that she did not have to. She had a choice, and that's why it's important that we understand two things. First, that our call comes with a choice. Second, we must choose to call out that pain. We must choose to respond to God's call on our lives, even with all the pain and uncertainty it brings. The woman with the issue called out that pain and said to herself, "Today is the day that I will reach out and get my healing." When she decided that she was fed up with her issue and had done all she could do physically and financially, she made a choice to get in the presence of Jesus.

That one touch changed her life instantly. I declare this as confirmation that there was a purpose already attached to you at birth, like your birthmark. No matter what life looked or felt like growing up, you have always been under the grace of God. There comes a time when you must step into everything that is already within you. As I begin to step into purpose, I am in awe at how naturally it flows. When the woman touched Jesus, I am sure she was amazed at how fast the flow of blood stopped. The amazing thing about being under the grace of God is that he has already equipped you to overcome anything that comes up against you. The heaviness of the flow or the length of the flow of blood could not stand against the power of just one touch on the hem of Jesus' garment.

Did you catch that last sentence? Let me make it personal for you. No pain that you have experienced can stand up against the power of Jesus to heal your mind, body, or heart. You have access to his healing power. Jesus gave the woman power and healing because of her faith. Do you have the faith to press through all the crowdedness in your life—physically and mentally? Unlike the woman with the issue who only had one show and didn't know if or when Jesus would be in the area again, you have unrestricted access to his garment. I dare you to reach out and touch him.

From Blind to Believer

As a kid, I remember reading about Jesus healing all kinds of people as he preached from city to city. It began to seem like nothing special and more like his job. About three years ago, my friend and I started doing morning wake-up calls. During the calls, we would take turns doing a mini-Bible lesson and praying with each other. One of my first lessons was on the story of the blind man. When I think about making peace with my own process, this is one of the first stories that spoke to me.

The story of the blind man is told in the ninth chapter of John. When Jesus and the disciples came across the man born blind, the disciples asked, "Rabbi, who sinned, this man or his parents, that he was born blind?" It was a cultural belief that sin led to issues and punishment—much like what we call karma and generational curses today—but Jesus cleared it up by letting them know that the man was born blind so that the works of God could be seen through him. Then, he spit on the ground, made some mud, placed it on the man's eyes and told him to go wash his eyes in the Pool of Siloam. The man followed Jesus' instructions and went home with his sight.

The neighbors did not believe it was him at first. They asked him who had given him his sight. He explained what Jesus had done. Then, they asked him where Jesus was, but he didn't know. They even took him to the Pharisees to investigate his healing. He explained what had occurred, and some believed him while others didn't. They even sent for his parents to confirm that he was their child, born blind, and could now see. Even with him and his parents' testimony, they still shunned him and threw him out.

This story is very critical to me making peace with my mother and father's deaths when I was young. For years, I wondered why I had to endure such losses while I had friends with parents. Was I cursed? Were my parents cursed? Like the disciples, I believed that something bad had to have caused me to be punished. It began to feel like a generational curse. I felt like I was destined to die young and leave my kids the same way I was left. As a Christian, I was ashamed to admit those feelings, but they were my truth. Even with all that I had overcome, it was hard for me to understand the purpose of the losses.

I didn't fully understand until Thanksgiving of 2017. I was sitting in church, listening to a therapist talk about dealing with death. She explained how important it is to grieve and be okay with not being okay. At the end of the presentation, she asked if anyone wanted to share their thoughts. I wanted to get up, but I felt paralyzed—physically and verbally—so, I just sat there and took it all in. It was that day that I realized that I had not properly grieved the loss of my parents. I know that last sentence sounds silly. How do you properly grieve? I didn't know the answer to that question, but I knew there was something missing. I left church that day an emotional wreck. Fifteen years' worth of pain masked in strength had resurfaced, and I could not run from it.

I knew that I had to make peace with this, but I didn't know how. Around 10 pm one night, I received a message on social media that read, "How did you deal with the death of your mom?" It was from someone I had a strained relationship within the past. We hadn't talked for about 3 years, but God had led her to me that night—for us to have an exchange. She had recently lost her son to a sudden crib death. My heart broke for her. I could feel her pain and her strength. She didn't even know it was strength yet. It took strength for her to reach out to me.

As I talked to her, God talked to me. This was the first time I really transitioned from pain to peace to prophecy. I was able to connect to her that night, because I had endured her pain. As we talked, I explained that I would not be able to have this conversation with her had I not endured the loss of my mother. Some disappointments were ordained because of my why. My parents, my broken marriage, and more were ordained and aligned to push me into my why. Even though they felt like death sentences at the time it happened, I look back at them and feel strong and accomplished because I not only survived but I get to share and support others.

I was at training one weekend. One of my co-workers requested for me to come to his office to assist with a soldier who was crying. When I walked in, I knew who it was and what it was. My heart dropped, and I immediately got a lump in my throat. I was in uniform, and I didn't come here to cry. I have been a soldier for almost 14 years now, and this moment took me back to who I was fourteen years ago—broken and confused, walking around with a strong physical presence but mentally weak. I was living off prayers and only in my right mind by the grace of God.

It was amazing how much we had in common that she had no clue about. She had a son the same age as mine. She had lost his father to violence before he was even born. As if being a single parent at 17 years old wasn't hard enough, she had recently lost her mother, and her brother was still recovering from gunshot wounds. To top it off, she was leaving for training in a few weeks with little time to process all of this, and this Sunday at drill, it all seemed to come down on her. I just sat beside her on the couch and hugged her tightly. As I hugged her, I could feel the strength in that little 115-pound body.

I couldn't help the tears from falling. I understood her. Like me, she felt cheated and undeserving of the hand she had been dealt in life. While she knew where her strength came from, she didn't understand why she had to be the strong one. I explained that I had lost my dad before knowing him, and my mom died in a car accident when I was just 17 years old, and, that I was also a mother of two kids who I've had to make sacrifices to provide for. I told her, I didn't always understand why, but God always had my back and made a way for me. We laughed, and we cried.

I was only able to sit there in that moment with her, because I had been her, and, one day, she would be me to someone else, and, the torch could continue. See, like the blind man, I had been chosen so that God's glory could be seen in me, so that she could see that this was only the beginning of what she is destined to achieve, if she stayed the course. I knew she was chosen, and God had something special for her, because he had been faithful to me, despite all that I had been through. People used to tell me how strong I was and how they could not imagine what I had been through. This angered me, because I wished I could not imagine either, but instead, my head was filled with images, and my heart was left with a void. I never asked to be the poster of strength. I would have taken the ideal childhood any day, but being able to not only encourage her, but also identify with her in that moment gave me a great sense of peace. To know that my pain had been purposed for this opportunity to prophesy was powerful to me.

I just had an aha moment while connecting my experiences with the story of the man born blind. In the beginning of writing, I mentioned that the scripture scared me when it read 'prophet' because I never imagined attaching that term to my name. It seemed a bit much for an ordinary woman like me. To help me get my thoughts organized and create an outline, I registered for a prophetic writing course, and it still didn't hit me. The information was very helpful in my writing, and it made sense, but the term was still too much for me. I remember sharing some information with my friend who is also writing, and she expressed the same feelings. We laughed at ourselves. Now that I am at the place of "making peace with the process," it has really hit me. Everyone is called to be a prophet, which is to profess or proclaim the will of God through their lives. I am a prophet. You are a prophet. We are prophets. Everyone has a story or a 'thing' that God has placed in their life for them to fulfill his will. My 'thing' is the loss of my parents at a young age. My issue became my influence the day I began to look at it differently.

The disciples questioned the cause of his blindness, while the people questioned the cure. They were interested in who had granted the man his sight. His physical blindness opened their spiritual eyes as he became a witness to the miraculous power Jesus possessed. I realized that my experiences as a child and my role as a military recruiter and youth mentor were way deeper than the numerical mission assigned to me. The moments when I feel most fulfilled are not tied to my work at all. I had been chosen for this role before I was born, just like the man was born blind. I experienced certain things to prepare me for this role.

The funny thing about the girl at drill is that she is from my hometown. I remember seeing her on social media when she was pregnant with her son. She moved away, and we ended up seeing each other at drill almost two years later—not by coincidence, but by the will of God. I had no idea that I would get to prophesy to her that day. The message I received on Facebook years later was totally unexpected. I had not spoken to that person in three years. She reached out to me—not by coincidence, but by the will of God. Now I understand what Habakkuk 2:3 says about the vision being for an appointed time and thought it may be delayed, but it will come to pass.

I had to make peace with my pain in order to fulfill my purpose that day. The beautiful thing about this call is that every time I get to answer it, I get more peace with the process. As I pour into others, God refuels me with more peace, passion, and purpose. I also know that I have planted a seed in them that will grow. One day, each of them will get to share their story and pour into someone else. It is like a domino effect. Imagine the lives that will be touched for many generations to come as we all answer our call to prophesy.

Each one of these stories adds valuable insight to my journey from pain to peace to prophecy. Esther and Joseph traveled different paths of pain, but both possessed a purpose that saved their people. Esther, the one of unknown favor, chose to step out of fear in faith when she approached the king on the behalf of her people. Joseph, the golden child, knew he was chosen long before his chance came, but he chose to ride the rollercoaster from the prison to the palace. The woman with the issue could have lived hidden in shame, but she pursued Jesus, understanding that he possessed her healing. The man born blind cried out to Jesus for his sight, and once he received it, he became a prophet to the people.

I can attest that sometimes I've felt as abandoned as Esther, and others, I've felt destined for greatness like Joseph. I've seen things come to pass only after what felt like years of pain. I've had issues for which I've had to cry out to God because no one else could fix them. I've lived with pain I felt cursed to bear until I realized I was chosen to carry the torch. While each of these times brought about different emotions, I can look back in peace, knowing that the same God was with me through it all. He never left my side, despite my feelings, and, being able to write these words to you is proof that eventually all roads—whether winding, bumpy, or smooth—will lead to prophecy.

You must understand that God ordained every moment in your life to fit into the fulfillment of his will. You aren't just co-incidentally going through life just to get to death. Just because you survive everything life has thrown at you doesn't mean you have won. Your survival does not serve its spiritual purpose if God doesn't get to use you. You still have levels of glory that you cannot touch until you understand, accept, and answer your call to prophesy—for you and for others. What if Esther, Joseph, the woman with the issue, or the blind mad had been silent or still in their moments of prophecy? I cannot imagine how the story would have unfolded. Not only that, but I needed these stories to understand my strength and make peace with the process. Now, you must understand this:

1. When you make peace with the fact that there is a process and a purpose, you can be still and let God work miracles.

2. When you make peace with the process, you can let that bitterness go, with the understanding that you were created for better.

3. When you make peace with the process, you can understand that those places where you felt undeserving were designed to prepare you for your destiny.

4. When you make peace with the process, you understand that those things you survived were not meant for just your success, but for you to share so that others can see God's work.

I'm not just talking to encourage you; I have seen his work with my own eyes. Let's go back to one of the areas where I felt cheated. My mother died on the morning of my ballet recital. I had danced for 10 years, and this is what God throws at me on the day I had prepared for all year. Cheated was a nice way to define the anger I felt; so, when my aunt asked me about praise dancing, it was an automatic "no". I didn't owe her an explanation, either. What was she thinking? Was she not there that morning with me crying on the side of the road? Had she not taken me to the dance recital, only for my instructor to call my name and request prayers for our family? Now, she wanted me to "praise dance", but there was no praise in my dance.

Sorry, but those were my honest feelings for a long time. I didn't make peace with the pain of dancing for the God who took my mother away on the morning of my dance recital until I was in Iraq. In 2008, I was deployed to Baghdad, Iraq. I attended a multicultural gospel service on Sundays. A few soldiers and I formed a praise dance team, and I danced and fell in love with dance all over again. On New Year's Eve, I gave a testimony of my experiences with dance, and we danced to "Never Would

Have Made It" by Marvin Sapp. As I danced and cried, I shed many years of weighed down resentment and bitterness.

Dancing with my battle buddies in that foreign place felt perfect. It was as if God had taken me away from my comfort zone to confront my issues. It was there that one of the most painful experiences in my life had turned into my place of praise. I have danced myself out of some dark places in life. What I was once told I needed therapy for, became therapeutic. It came natural to me. I didn't choose dance. God chose dance for me. I've been dancing ever since.

I told you that your call is connected to others, and we see how Joseph's call changed the course of his family history. One thing that has been heavy on my mind is leaving a legacy for my children. My friends and I talk about financial security, but also about leaving them with something intangible. My daughter has a lot of my personality and skills, so, you know I was excited to enroll her in dance lessons. It comes natural to her, and she loves it. I am amazed at how she learns and choreographs dances at her young age. She is so mature, that I am careful of the type of dances that I expose her to.

On Easter Sunday, I stood in the back of the church and watched my 6-year-old daughter praise dance. She looked like an angel. As I recorded her, my hand shook, and tears formed in my eyes. As beautiful as she danced, those few minutes took me down memory lane. I was reminded of the little girl who loved to dance, the teenager who lost her mother the morning of her dance recital, and the young woman who had no desire to praise God through dance, but by the grace of God, had found her way back to dancing—not just dancing, but praise dancing. When I began dancing, I never imagined having a daughter and being able to watch her dance; and just before the song ended, I heard God say, "Your legacy begins. Your blessing was in your obedience."

For God to get the glory, I had to let go of the hurt I associated with dancing and embrace it as a method of praise. When I began dancing, I began ministering to and connecting with others. I began to understand my purpose and make peace with the process. Watching my baby dance is confirmation that God chose each of us before we were born. She had no idea, but I can feel the spirit of God when she dances. I can see lives being touched, strongholds being broken, and power being released as she grows into her gift. It's a nervous sense of excitement, knowing that I have been chosen as the caretaker of this gift. I am responsible for covering and conditioning her to operate in her gift.

I know that God spoke to me through her, because I received peace and a refreshed passion for working with the youth praise dancers. God chose this task for me before I was born. He called me into it as a child. Even though I experienced challenges, he never left me; and for his faithfulness, I am committed to his work. My call is connected to not only my baby, but to generations to come. This legacy will outlive me.

Making peace with this process has been a journey for me. Before I began writing this book, I didn't fully understand the purpose of the process. As I poured my heart into these pages and marinated on the word of God, God literally walked me from pain to peace to prophecy. This book has written itself one page at a time. There were sections that wrote themselves naturally, because the words were already in me, waiting to flow out of me. There were sections I wanted to zoom past to avoid the emotions that resurfaced. God made me sit in some stuff until I got the understanding and peace I needed.

What I am trying to convey is the fact that God can use you, even in your brokenness, confusion, and flaws, if you are willing to commit to being used by him. The places where you felt cheated will always be there. Making peace with the process doesn't erase those painful memories or unfavorable circumstances. You must continuously speak life into those areas that try to take you out. Reality is, peace is a process. I know this, because there are some areas in my life that require maintenance to maintain my mindset.

It's easy to say, "My issue became my influence," but, to walk like it, talk like it, and live like it is another level of peace. I remember calling someone about a disagreement I was having with my son's father. I was boiling HOT. When I was done with my rant, he said, "I have no sympathy for you in that situation. You knew what you were getting into. You made that bed, so put your big-girl panties on, and get over it." With tears in my eyes, all I could say was, "Okay." He had broken me down to size in three sentences. I was hurt, but the next thing he said changed my mindset. He told me, "Act like you know who you are. You said God is going to bless you with what you want. Stop acting like you don't believe what you said."

Those words meant more to me than he understood. Whereas his first response chopped me down, the second one snapped me back together instantly. I realized that I had been speaking stuff that I really wasn't believing. When I began to shift from just speaking over that struggle to operating like I knew what I was speaking, the more peace I possessed. The more peace I possessed, the more I saw the promises of God manifest in my life.

My question for you is, are you making peace or just making progress? Yes, there is a difference. For years, I made progress, but not peace. Progress had me chasing personal goals, but peace pushed me into purpose. Now, I am pushing you. Have you made peace with your past in preparation for your prophetic future? Everything that Esther, Joseph, the blind man, and the woman with the issue experienced showed how God's unfailing loves never faded, and his plan was ultimately fulfilled through their lives. Everything that you have experienced, the scars you carry, the peace you have gained, and the power you possess, are what call and qualify you to step into your prophetic role. You haven't made it to this point in this book by chance, but by choice. Now, let's take the next step.

NOT CHEATED, BUT CHOSEN

Chapter Six
Stepping in Your Prophetic Role

Everyone has their own destiny. Not everyone makes the choice to follow it. Reality is, we exist for God's purpose. He has chosen each one of us to serve him in our own special way. He has equipped us with the exact personality and body to do the work he has chosen us for. The Holy Spirit has gifted us with the spiritual gifts to serve once we answer the call. In those moments where we are waiting on God to step in, he is often waiting on us to step out. We must step out in faith and obedience, knowing that.

1. God chose us before we were born.
2. Being called comes with a choice that we must make.
3. Being called doesn't exempt us from the enemy's attack.
4. Calling out those painful areas where you feel cheated cuts off the enemy's access.
5. Making peace with the process strengthens your steps.

Understanding that I am chosen, answering my call, calling out my pain, and making peace with the process should allow me to confidently walk in my prophetic role. I just used the word 'should' because I have been stuck in the same section for about two weeks. I initially attributed it to my busy schedule and writer's block. Reality is, I couldn't write about what I wasn't ready to do. Writing this book has been a therapeutic release. Getting to this point should be exciting, but I am secretly terrified.

Earlier I discussed how the devil would insert a painful memory in every happy moment in my life and try to disqualify me based on my past and current circumstances. He tried me. As I come to this last chapter in the book, the thought of me being an author has set in. I took headshots two weeks ago and sent the cover image, summary, and author's bio to the graphic designer. I began making plans for a release event. I am excited, and the enemy is mad—so mad, he has been riding on my trail, trying to stop me. What he doesn't understand is, I am still going to STEP.

My prophetic role is not about anything to the left and right of me, but everything to the front and back of me. Everything that has occurred in my life has prepared me for this role. Isaiah 55: 10-13 reads:

"The rain and snow come down from the heavens and stay on the ground to water the earth. They cause the grain to grow, producing seed for the farmer and bread for the hungry. It is the same with my word. I sent it out, and it will prosper everywhere I send it. You will live in joy and peace. The mountains and hills will burst into a song, and the trees of the field will clap their hands! Where there were thorns, cypress trees will grow. Where nettles grew, myrtles will sprout up. These events will bring great honor to the Lord's name; they will be an everlasting sign of his power and love."

This scripture speaks to the little girl in me that feels called to produce great fruit but is crippled by past pains and failures. In the middle of this scripture, God said, "It will prosper every-where I send it." This sentence alone lets me know two things. First, there is nowhere I can go that will take me out of the will of God. Second, God has already gone ahead of me and set the atmosphere of prosperity. These two things qualify me and you to boldly proclaim the will of God through our lives.

When I looked at the rain and snow as my own experiences, it began to strengthen my steps. Since God chose me, everything I have experienced—good and bad—was chosen for me for the purpose assigned to me. Just as the rain and snow water the earth, so does my story, so does your story. Your life is your living testimony. Your struggles, trials, setbacks, comebacks, and everything you have experienced stay in your life to water the ground you walk on. It causes your FAITH to grow, produces your TESTIMONY, and provides a PROPHETIC WORD for you to share with God's people.

Sharing the word of God with others can be relatively easy. I knew how to quote scriptures as a child. In fact, my daughter has been able to speak the word of God since she was just four years old. We were lying in bed one night, and she looked over at me and said, "Don't give up on God. God will never give up on you. He will give you whatever you want." I don't know what she had asked God for and he had given her or how she knew that Mommy needed that word at that moment. What I did know was that God had spoken to me through my child, and, if she could speak the prophetic word of God with just her four years of experience, surely you have not only a word, but can bear witness to wonderful works of God.

God created you on purpose and ordained every detail of your life to fit into your prophetic role. He creates in you everything needed to fulfill your purpose. He chose your parents and your pathway. Even when you feel like you are failing, God's will is prevailing. Even when you feel undeserving, know that you are still destined for greatness. God does not reverse or cancel the call on your life. You can never make enough mistakes to disqualify you. You can never make enough wrong turns to miss out on your turn. In fact, God qualifies who he calls. The story of Isaiah demonstrates the call, choice, cleansing, and commitment process of those called by God. Isaiah was a reputable scribe by trade, but God had chosen him for the very special task of being a prophet. God came to Isaiah in a vision. In the vision, there were angels attending to God. Not just any angels; these were seraphim. These angels represented perfection, holiness, and purity. Isaiah was delighted and devastated at the same time. In Isaiah 6:58 he responds saying:

Then I said, "It's all over! I am doomed, for I am a sinful man. I have filthy lips, and I live among a people with filthy lips. Yet, I have seen the King, the Lord of Heaven's Armies." Then one of the seraphim flew to me with the burning coal he had taken from the altar with a pair of tongs. He touched my lips with it and said, "See, this coal has touched your lips. Now, your guilt is removed, and your sins are forgiven." Then I heard the Lord asking, "Whom should I send as a messenger to the people? Who will go for us?" I said, "Here I am. Send me."

The clearer Isaiah's vision became the more he was aware of not only God's strength, but his imperfections and inadequacy, as well. He knew he wasn't qualified, yet God and the angels had appeared to him. The key word is 'yet' which means that even amid his shortcomings, he was chosen. Because he acknowledged his sins, he was also forgiven. The cleansing process was essential to his role as a prophet. Just one touch of the hot coal combined with his confession was enough to hear the words, *'Your sins are forgiven'.*

I can imagine how much lighter Isaiah felt after hearing those words. Being lighter made it easier for him to answer the call.

Understanding Isaiah's transition from scribe to prophet makes it easier for me and you to step. When God called, Isaiah answered immediately. Are you ready to say, "Send me"? Are you ready to be a messenger to the people? Of course, you are. You have not arrived at this section, to sit down. It is time for you to STEP.

Step One: Forgive Yourself and Others

"And when you stand praying, if you hold anything against anyone, forgive them, so that your Father in heaven may forgive you your sins" (Mark 11:25).

"Then he adds: 'Their sins and lawless acts I will remember no more'" (Hebrews 10:17).

As I sat in the nail salon chair getting a pedicure, I decided to grab my notebook and write. I wrote down the things I needed to forgive myself for and a few things I needed to forgive others for. Like you, I have been harboring some feelings of unforgiveness and resentment. While I claimed to use them to give me extra motivation, reality is, they held more negative power than I acknowledged. I had a long list, so I will share my top five things I had to forgive myself and others for.

1. There was absolutely nothing that I could have done to prevent my mother from dying that day. Being in the car would not have made a difference. Being a better daughter would not have made a difference. It was God's plan.

2. I forgive the woman in the other car that collided with my mother's car. I never met her; but I've been angry with her. Unsure of what happened, I automatically blamed her, because she lived. It wasn't her fault. It was God's plan.

3. I forgive myself for leaving the security of my career for an unhealthy marriage. I knew it was unstable, and I

risked it all and ended up back in my hometown on my auntie's couch with my one-year-old daughter to care for. Even though I have been blessed with an amazing support system that I could not imagine raising my kids without, and I've been back in the military full-time for almost five years, I still have this soft spot of regret. That spot of regret turns to forgiveness today. It was God's plan.

4. I forgive myself for staying in relationships longer than necessary. I was a builder who got burned out and bitter when the project didn't follow the blueprint. I forgive myself for investing more in building others than myself. I forgive others for not living up to my expectations. I take the lessons learned and the love shared as part of my process. It will all fit into God's perfect will for my life.

5. I forgive myself for not stepping into my prophetic role earlier in life. I battled with feeling unqualified and unprepared for years, and here I am at the end of my first book. What I put off for years, has written itself in five months. The biggest blessing is the release and peace that I've gained. While I may feel delayed, I know that God's timing is perfect, and this is only the beginning.

An adage says, "Forgiveness is for you, not the other person." Forgiving oneself and others is the beginning step of walking in favor. Joseph understood the meaning of forgiveness. He could have capitalized on his brothers' need for him and their remorse for what they had done to him. Instead, he forgave them and welcomed them in. In fact, during the 20-plus years he was without his family, you never hear of him mentioning how they had sold him into slavery. He showed no signs of bitterness. What he did show signs of was favor, and in the end, his favor put him in the position to save his family, transferring the favor to them for many generations to come. Now, imagine if he had harbored unforgiveness and resentment towards them.

I wonder what drew the connection between Joseph's position to his purpose. How did he know that God had sent him ahead of his family so that he could save them? His forgiving heart, strength and his family success are confirmation for me and you. Just look back at some of the events that have played out in our lives. I can recall many moments where the cliché, "What the devil meant for evil God turned around for my good," is so true. Those five things I had to forgive myself for are just a few of my moments.

The key is not to be able to look back with forgiveness. The key is to look around and ahead in forgiveness, with the understanding that God has a purpose, and everything we experience is connected to our prophetic role. I believe that Joseph's heart was fixed on God's favor and not his brothers' failure. He forgave them before he was reunited with them. That is how he was able to walk in favor and win all the way around. Truth is, we don't need to see the end to know that we will win, so, why hold grudges, bitterness and resentment for victories you have already won? If you are, you need to stop today.

You are NOT your past mistakes or struggles. You are NOT the generational curses passed down to you. You have been chosen to be the breakthrough that will make a lie out of everything determined to break you. Forgive yourself for thinking less of yourself. Forgive yourself for allowing others to make you bitter and resentful. Even hanging on a cross to be crucified with two thieves, Jesus said, "Father, forgive them, for they do not know what they do." When they hung him and laid him in the tomb, they had no idea that he would rise in triumph and testimony. They had no idea that it was all for them.

We are not like them. We know that he did it all for us. He was thinking of us and forgave us before we ever sinned. How can we accept his forgiveness and favor without extending it to others? How can we expect to be forgiven unless we forgive? We are all imperfect human beings living by the grace of God's perfect will. He chose us, and we must choose forgiveness — for others, for ourselves and for our prophetic role. Joseph could not do it with resentment and bitterness. I realized that I could not even finish this section of the book without it. It's your time.

Step Two: Own Your Struggles

Remember, dear brothers and sisters, that few of you were wise in the world's eyes or powerful or wealthy when God called you. Instead, God chose things the world considers foolish in order to shame those who think they are wise. And he chose things that are powerless to shame those who are powerful. God chose things despised by the world, things counted as nothing at all, and used them to bring to nothing what the world considers important. 1 Corinthians 1:26-28

I didn't come to this section like Joseph, free of unforgiveness. I had to make peace with the process. I did come into this like Isaiah — just amazed at how God had chosen a little flawed flower like me to bloom into a prophetic writer. I know that I am not the model Christian, and I never received the People's Choice Award. When I heard the prophet speak of me writing a book, I was tickled. I remember joking about it on the way home. Whereas much of what was said to me that day was true, some of it felt a bit off target.

I wondered what fool would think of me as a Christian author. When I began writing, I was very careful only to discuss my work with those who I felt were going to be supportive. I hid my plan from those who could possibly question my purpose and validate my insecurities. The people who supported and encouraged me probably had no idea I was secretly terrified. The more I wrote, the more God revealed to me that I was in the right place. On days I felt like a fool, he showed me favor. I can admit this has been my biggest struggle throughout the entire writing process. The words came naturally, but my confidence and faith came slowly.

As I own my struggle and push towards the finish line, I am reminded of Jesus, who came as a humble, poor servant and offered his life for our chance at eternal life. He lived amongst the world and experienced our struggles. They doubted him. They judged him. They discredited him. They considered him and his work foolish; yet, he healed the sick, gave sight to the blind, saved many from death, and much more. They crucified him and made mockery of him hanging on the cross, unable to save himself. At that time, only a fool would have believed he would rise again in three days; yet, he did. His suffering and his success set the standard for you and me.

One morning on the way to work, I was listening to a Sarah Jakes Roberts sermon, and she referenced the scripture used above. The title of the sermon was "Foolish Glory". I listened to that same podcast three times that day. I saved the scripture to come back to it. It spoke to the fool in me trying to walk in all the favor that God was pouring into my life. I realized three things that I must share with you.

1. *It is okay to feel like a fool.* You don't have to be perfect to have purpose. In fact, God wants to use the foolish things

you and I have done, to show the world just how powerful his purpose is. We no longer must be ashamed of our past failures or present circumstances. We no longer must wait until we get past our 'foolish' state of life for everyone to forget what a "fool" we have been. God CHOSE the foolish things that the people count as useless and unqualified, to bring GLORY to God

2. *It is okay to be considered a fool in the world's eyes.* The scripture says that God is going to use the foolish things to bring shame to those who think they are wise and powerful. I'd rather be a fool in God's favor than wise in the world. What the people of the world think of us is not our concern. We need no validation or justification from them to be used by God. Jesus' crucifixion and resurrection are the most profound examples of foolish glory and the only ones we need to understand our purpose and God's power.

3. *God's glory is going to come from this fool.* For everyone in the world who sees you as a fool, someone will see God in you. Someone's breakthrough is connected to your purpose. I struggled with writing this book, wondering who would read it. I struggled publishing this book, wondering how I would pay for it; and if no one reads it but you, God will receive his glory from this fool, because I know this — I have never been so proud to be called a 'fool'.

I own my struggles of feeling cheated, unqualified, and foolish, yet chosen. It's time you do the same. There is something inside you awaiting the fool in you to come forth. There is something waiting on you to own your struggles and move forward in strength. There is hidden glory in your story — glory that was planted in you before you were born. God has been birthing prophets since the beginning of Earth. As we receive and release prophecy through our lives, we call out purpose in others. Purposes from Heaven are manifested on Earth when called people come forth. Look how many lives were saved when Esther and Joseph owned their struggles. One was an orphan and the other a slave and prisoner. Both understood they were chosen and chose to walk in their prophetic role. Will you?

Step Three: Shift Your Mindset

Earlier in the book, I mentioned how God reveals things to me at the most random times. I got this revelation a couple months ago and could not figure out what it was about. One Sunday morning, I was sitting on my daughter's bed, combing her hair before church. She was watching the Disney channel. She blurted out, "Mama, I am going to be strong like Moana." I don't watch much tv except HGTV, so I had no idea what she was referring to, so, I began to watch the movie with her. It was so good; I almost didn't make it to church. God was just dropping nuggets in my spirit. I was like, "Really, God? I am writing a book based on your word, and you want me to talk about a Disney movie?"

Yes, he wanted me to talk about a Disney movie. Pressing for time, I wrote down what I had for later. Over the next few days, I watched clips and took notes. It felt like an intimate conversation with God. I have been holding it in my notes for the right time to share it with you. There were a few places I wanted to insert it, and I tried. However, I would get frustrated, because it didn't make sense, and erase it.

Truth is, this section has been one of the hardest ones for me to process. I've been sitting here for days feeling off-balance. It is no secret that I have been secretly terrified of my call. I've owned my struggles and accepted the fact that I am a favored fool, but what's next? I've written a whole book, and I am excited about it, but what is next for me and the world who is going to read it? How will we make the transition from understanding our call to stepping into our prophetic role?

This is when God said, "You have to shift your mindset," and I respond, "I hear you, but I'm not understanding what you want me to do." When I have my frustrating moments like this, I always go back to the title of the book — *Not Cheated, but Chosen*.

I remember disliking the word -but . In my younger days, I would quickly respond to others with, "Don't say 'but' to me. 'But' erases everything you said before that."

"I love you, but…"

"Your cooking tastes good, but…"

"Your interview was great, but…"

None of those ever felt good.

Now, let's say the title of the book together — *Not Cheated, but Chosen*. The three-letter word -but- sitting between the words 'Cheated' and 'Chosen' is the game-changer. Once you say "but", you can erase those feelings you have been holding onto. You are not your heartbreaks and broken relationships. You are not your anger, sadness and depression. You are not your sickness, pain, or setbacks. You are not your insecurities, fears, or doubts. Those feelings no longer have power. The word 'but' stripped them of the power they thought they had over your future. The only thing that is important is the word, CHOSEN! Because God chose you, there are no more 'buts' in your life. You stand confidently and unapologetically flawed and favored, and there is nothing anyone can do about it. You are limitless. Let me say this to myself, "I am limitless." We are limitless.

I finally understand the connection between the shift and the movie "Moana". If you have not seen the movie, let me go ahead and say this—spoiler alert! I cannot keep it to myself. Moana tells the story of a young girl called to restore the prosperity of her island. Moana felt called to the ocean from a child. While she was terrified of the unknown and felt unqualified, she longed to see what was beyond the boundaries of her village. The irony in her longing is that she was already on the path to becoming a chief. Her father, Tui, was a chief and often told Moana that she would be chief one day. My initial question was, with a confirmed inheritance, why does Moana feel called out of her comfort zone?

Last year, I shifted my focus to becoming a commissioned officer in the military. I am fully qualified and have been just waiting for the opportunity to present itself. I even reached out to a few people for assistance. I figured if I was going to retire, I might as well take advantage of the opportunity and make the most out of my service. I put my name out there and just waited. Well, a couple months ago, the door opened. I wanted to, and I had plenty of supporters encouraging me to do it. However, I could not follow through with it.

I battled with it for weeks—chase yet another military title or chase my purpose. I just felt like God was calling me out of my comfort zone into another realm of purpose. I started this year off with a plan to complete this book and become a certified career coach. I knew that becoming an officer was only my idea for the title and pay increase. This call to prophesy was so much more. I have dreams of my own career/life coaching business. I see the faces of those I am called to help, and even though I still have no idea how it will all play out, I can identify with Moana's feeling of being called into an ocean of unknowns.

Moana had her moments of doubt, but she remained strong and faithful to her mission. Her parents didn't want her to go, but she answered her call. She didn't even know how to sail, but she answered her call. She was met with turbulence and was initially thrown back to shore, but she kept going. She was no match for the feared giant named Maui, but she stood up to him. When she first met him, she said, "I am Moana of Tui. You will board my boat, sail across the sea, and restore the heart of Te Fiti." She had the mindset of a winner, no matter the size of her opponent.

The story of Moana hit home for me in several ways. My two favorite quotes from her are, "Sometimes our strengths lie beneath the surface—far beneath in some cases," and "The ocean chose me for a reason." That Sunday morning was the first time I told my daughter that I was writing a book. Her immediate response was, "Really, Mommy? I'm going to write a book, too." She had no idea that I had no idea how I was going to accomplish this task. All she knew was, I was going to do it, and she could, too.

My daughter saw no boundaries. She is only six years old and is in her beginning reading stage. That tells me that we were born with her mindset. We weren't created feeling cheated. Life experiences planted that seed in our minds. It is time we shift back to our core—the core created by God before we were born so that we can fulfill our prophetic role. We were created to feel chosen. Like Moana, the ocean (God) chose us for a reason. Our strength lies in the core of what he created us to be—prophets to the nations.

Watching Moana and having a conversation with my daughter that morning played a key role in the shifting of my mindset. Once I told her what I was doing, I could not let her down. A few days ago, I was lying in bed, writing, and she came in my room. She leaned over the computer screen and began reading my work. I usually need my peace and space to write, but I read a few lines to her before showing her the word count. She said, "Wow, Mommy. That is a lot of words," and, it hit me. I had come a long way from that Sunday we were watching "Moana" because I shifted my mindset from a possibility to a promise, because my purpose is connected to her possibilities.

What type of mindset are you operating in? Are you playing it safe or are you ready to shift beyond your comfort zone into your prophetic role. Moana's longing seemed simple in the beginning, but she was the one chosen to restore the value of her family. Writing a book initially seemed like a great personal goal, but the goal is to fulfill God's will and leave a legacy for my kids. Neither of us could have accomplished our goal without a shift in our mindset. Are you willing to shift from playing safe to fulfilling prophecy?

Step Four: Build Your Strength

This writing process has taught me the real meaning of having an intimate relationship with God. When I committed to writing this book, I told God, "If you want me to do this, you are going to have to send me some help." I didn't know where the content would come from, how I would get it published, or who would read it. Remembering what the prophet said in 2016, I just opened a Word document and started typing. Each day, as God poured into me, I became stronger — mentally and spiritually. I became conditioned for my call. God spoke to me in three key forms: Direct Revelation, the Word of God, and Circumstances.

Direct Revelation

When I first began writing this book, God and I had a regular 3 a.m. purpose meeting. I would wake out of what felt like a deep sleep to write. I carried around this journal with me, and when God revealed stuff to me, I wrote it down. I downloaded an app that would allow me to talk while it typed. I talked to myself on my hour commute to work and emailed the documents to myself. God spoke to me through songs, sermons, tv shows, and anything else that he saw fit. I have never felt so connected to him in my life. I know that my intimate connection comes from my willingness to answer my call to prophesy. Take a minute to access your relationship with God's voice. Can you hear him speaking to you?

The Word of God

I never payed attention to how much God speaks to me through his word until I began writing this book. I have over 50 notes on my phone from sermons and scriptures. I keep them to refer to when I need them. I have needed them throughout this process. There are resources for individuals with writer's block. My resource was his word. Much of this book wrote itself long before I began writing it. The powerful thing about the word of God is that it never loses its power. Notes from over a year ago were often read like they were preached today.

It is amazing how God sends his word to me right when I need it. I am literally sitting on my bed, writing, and I just received a text message from my cousin with sermon notes from today. Four sentences stood out to me:

1. How important it is to hear what God says.
2. Whatever God tells you to do, you do it.

3. All in God's timing, when he gets ready for you to be where he wants you to be, He will make it happen.

4. God will cause your situation to speak to you.

I sent back a screenshot of where I was typing in the book in our group message to show the significance of that message. Those statements confirm the value of building an intimate relationship with God by studying his word and listening to his voice. More important to me, they confirm just how faithful God has been in sending me help along this journey. This section wrote itself in another city through a pastor I have never heard preach. The power of purpose, connection and position is real. I am still amazed. Do you understand the purpose of the word of God? Are you connected to people who can speak a word over you? Are you in position — mentally and physically — to receive and release a word?

Circumstances

If you only learn one thing about me, I want you to know this: My life has taught me that God is real. Like the woman with the issue of blood, there have been some issues in my life that I would not have survived without pressing my way to God. While some of my struggles have felt like the end of the world, the influence that they gave me has been unexplainable. Losing my parents at an early age was very hard; however, being able to witness to others during their time of bereavement is a blessing. Being an unmarried career woman with two children was not part of my plan. However, being an inspiration and encouragement to others trying to accept and balance this position is a blessing. I would not be writing a book titled, *Not Cheated, but Chosen*, had I not experienced circumstances where I felt cheated. I have a long list of examples, but I don't even need it. The proof is in the pain, peace, and prophecy.

Every time you survive what was expected to take you out, your story gets stronger. Like a boxer, every round of every fight conditions you for your prophetic role. Sharing scriptures and the word of God is great, but your testimony hits differently. I don't remember much of the sermon from the Sunday my pastor talked about being favored in unfavorable circumstances. What I remember the most and what gave me the peace I longed for was her testimony. We shared that moment, and I will never forget it. Your circumstances give you the same strength. Your story and the story of those called and connected to you, are your assurance that you are chosen. All you must do is step.

I am not sure how strong your faith is; but I do know that the only way you can step into your prophetic role is by having an intimate relationship with God. God speaks to us in different ways so that we can hear his voice (direct revelation), feel his presence (his word), and know his power (our circumstances). Altogether, they are the perfect combination. Notice I said "perfect combination" and not just "perfect". There will be times your circumstances will leave you hungry for the word of God. There will be times your peace will only come from direct revelation. Just know that your strength comes from being chosen, and God conditions those he calls. You got this.

Step Five: Live in Favor

By now, you should KNOW that you were not cheated, but CHOSEN. It is no coincidence you have arrived at this section of this book. Like Mary, you were called to give birth to a child who will change the course of history. Like Esther, you were called to break generational curses and restore the strength of your bloodline. Like the woman with the issue of blood, you were chosen to show just how much healing power is in a step of faith in the right direction.

Like Joseph, God has revealed a plan for your life that will manifest at the appointed time, despite how many years it takes. Like the man born blind, you aren't suffering from the sins of you or your parents. Instead, you were chosen to be the vessel through which God's glory will shine. Just like God chose each of them, he chose you and me, so, there is no more room for feelings of being cheated. No more bitterness. No more pity parties. No more fear. There is no room for anything except—favor.

You can make peace with the fact that God chose ordinary people like you and me to fulfill his promises. You can forgive yourself for thinking you are anything less than God's imperfect prophet. You might as well own your struggles and shift your mindset. You were not cheated; you were chosen—not because I said you were chosen, but because God's word and your life have proven that you are. Your painful past is preparation for your prophetic future. Purpose called me, and I am calling you. It is time for you to live in the favor that was purchased and promised to you before you were formed in your mother's womb. As you step into your prophetic role, it is important that you understand-

Your calling is a GIFT from God.

Every good and perfect gift is from above, coming down from the Father of the heavenly lights, who does not change like shifting shadows. James 1:17

You are called for God's PURPOSE.

For we are God's handiwork, created in Christ Jesus to do good works, which God prepared in advance for us to do. Ephesians 2:10

God CHOSE your calling before you were born.

Before I formed you in your mother's womb, I chose you. Before you were born, I set you apart. I appointed you to be a prophet to the nations. Jeremiah 1:5

Your sins and mistakes DON'T CHANGE your calling.

And the God of all grace, who called you to his eternal glory in Christ, after you have suffered for a little while, will himself restore you and make you strong, firm and steadfast. 1 Peter 5:10

Your calling is PERMANENT.

For God's gifts and his call are irrevocable. Romans 11:29

Your calling is CONNECTED to others.

You are the light of the world. A town built on a hill cannot be hidden. Neither do people light a lamp and put it under a bowl. Instead they put it on its stand. In the same way, let your light shine before others, that they may see your good deed and glorify your Father in heaven. Matthew 5:14-16

God EMPOWERS you for what he calls you to do.

I have filled him with the Spirit of God, with wisdom, with under-standing, with knowledge and with all kinds of skills to make artistic designs for work in gold, silver and bronze, to cut and set stones, to work in wood, and to engage in all kinds of crafts. Exodus 31:3-5

There's a PRIZE for living your calling.

Therefore, my brothers and sisters, make every effort to confirm your calling and election. For if you do these things, you will never stumble. 2 Peter 1:10

Called people call people. Once I answered my call, I began to look at everyone around me differently. My purpose shifted from finding my own purpose to pulling out purpose. Where you see pain, I see purpose. I find peace in knowing that I was not cheated; I was chosen and, so were you. Every area of our lives was created for a purpose — a purpose assigned to us before we were formed in our mothers' wombs. A call to profess the powerful word of God through our testimony. I have answered my call. Here is the beginning of my testimony. I can't promise to be perfect, but I am committed. Are you?

Personal Reflection and Resolution

I am still in awe of God's faithfulness. Despite my fears and failures, he has been faithful. When I started this word document in January, I had no clue what this process or product would look or feel like. I always joke with my coworkers about having commitment anxiety. I thought that writing a book would take a long time, too long for me to commit to. Another writer changed my mindset. She said that when its prophetic writing, which is the words that God has given to you to release, it doesn't not take long. It is all about being available and being committed. Six months later as a career woman, mother of two, and as my family would say 'busy body', it is done.

Being able to fulfill what was prophesied over me in 2016 has solidified the meaning of the words 'I chose you' as spoken by God in Jeremiah 1:5. There is no way that I could have retraced my life and connected the my experiences to the word without God. When the prophet said others needed the hear the things I didn't want to talk about, she should have added that I needed to hear these those things too. I needed to release myself. My pastor once said that as a minister, she was the first to receive the word. Now, I understand what she meant. This book was for me too.

I have learned so much about myself. I am stronger than I ever thought I was because now I know where my strength comes from. I am more qualified than I ever thought I was because now I know who qualified me. I am more committed than I ever had been because I see the fruits of my labor. Not just the idea of being an author, but the favor that I have felt throughout this process. If I never make a penny, I have found peace and power in this process. Peace with my past and power in my future. Self- limits and boundaries have been removed. I am evolving into the woman God predestined me to be.

I have already committed to my call as a prophetic writer. I am scheduled to attend my first Southern Christian Writer's Conference this year. I have written down my next two projects on my vision board. This is only the beginning. I have tasted the power in my purpose and there is no way I can put it on pause. I have accepted these four affirmations and I challenged you to do the same.

1. I am chosen for a purpose that only I can fulfill.
2. Nothing happens by coincidence and nothing can cancel the call on my life.
3. My call is designed to bless others and glorify God.
4. I am not cheated, I am chosen. God chose me.

You are not cheated, you are chosen. God has gifted you with something for his glory. You are responsible for returning the gift back to him through prophesy. When I began writing, I was afraid of the word prophet. Now, I am honored to be chosen to be a prophet to all nations. I encourage you not to be afraid, but to be bold. Whatever you are called to do, do it. If you know what it is, stop doubting and start doing. If you don't know what it is, start praying and ask God to reveal it to you. Listen to that voice you hear when no one is talking; the nudge your feel when no one is around; the idea that keeps you up at night; the call you haven't answered. I leave you with these two scriptures.

"We have different gifts, according to the grace given to each of us. If your gift is prophesying, then prophesy in according with your faith; if it is serving, then serve; if it is teaching, then teach; if it is encouraging, then give encouragement; if it is giving, then give generously, if it is to lead, do it diligently; if it is show mercy, do it cheerfully." (Romans 12: 6-8)

"Each of you should use whatever gift you have received to serve others, as faithful stewards of God's grace in its various forms. If anyone speaks, they should do so as one who speaks the very words of God. If anyone serves, they should do so with the strength God provides, so that in all things God may be praised through Jesus Christ. To him be the glory and the power for ever and ever. Amen." (1 Peter 4: 10-11)

Your call has been confirmed. Your phone is ringing. I challenge you to answer it. Remember you were chosen for such a time as now. Now, the choice is yours. What will you choose?

About the Author

Desmicia Calhoun is a proud mother of two, a Soldier and an evolving woman of God. She has over thirteen years of military service and currently serves as an Army National Guard Guidance Counselor in Alabama. She earned a Bachelor of Arts in Organizational Management. She also earned a Master of Education in both Early Childhood Education Administration and Student Affairs in Higher Education.

Desmicia has a passion for helping others unpack their fears, pursue their purpose, and build a successful career. After chasing and accomplishing her personal and professional goals, she finally decided to answer her call to prophetic writing. This is the first of many books that will be birthed as Desmicia embraces her purpose.